How to Start a Business Analyst Career

A roadmap to start an IT career in business analysis

OR

How to find entry-level business analyst jobs

Laura Brandenburg

Many of the designations used by manufacturers and sellers to distinguish their products are claimed as trademarks. Where those designations appear in this book, and the author was aware of a trademark claim, the designations have been printed with initial capital letters or all in capitals.

The author has taken care in the preparation of this book but makes no expressed or implied warranty of any kind and assumes no responsibility for errors or omissions. No liability is assumed for incidental or consequential damages in connection with or arising out of the use of the information or programs contained herein.

ISBN 1450570801
EAN-13 9781450570800

Testimonials for

How to Start a Business Analyst Career

"There is no one path to becoming a Business Analyst. Laura's book helps you leverage what you have and succeed in this fast growing profession."

-Kathleen Barret, CEO, International Institute of Business Analysis®

"I wish I had this book last year when I was seeking information out about how to become a business analyst."

-Douglas Hill, Senior Business Analyst

"I just picked up your book and can't tell you how it has helped in a short amount of time.

-Paul Akerind, PMP

"How to Start a Business Analyst Career *does a good job of connecting the dots. It addressed many of the questions, issues, and concerns I had about the business analysis field. Very comprehensive and informative."*

-David Maynard, starting a new career as a business analyst

A thought-provoking introduction into the reality of today's business analyst. The potential or new business analyst will obtain an initial framework for future growth in this field."

-Pat Ferdinandi, Business Architect

"How to Start a Business Analyst Career *is a very thorough and well-thought handbook on what it takes to break into a career in business analysis. The definition of the role and description of what to expect as a BA are spot on. The networking piece is a particular gem."*

-Jonathan Babcock, Business Analyst and Blogger

Author Online

For more resources about starting and advancing your business analyst career, visit the author at

www.bridging-the-gap.com

For Further Help

Laura Brandenburg provides BA training, consulting, and mentoring services and works with a network of coaches, trainers, and mentors to help BAs build fulfilling careers in business analysis.

Laura offers an online course, Launching Your Business Analysis Career that takes students step-by-step through the process laid out in this book with online instructor support.

Check out *Bridging the Gap* for information about current offerings or contact Laura at info@bridging-the-gap.com for more details.

About the Author

Laura Brandenburg hosts *Bridging the Gap,* a blog to help business analysts advance their careers and is the founder of *My Business Analysis Career*, an online learning platform for business analysis professionals. Laura is passionate about the business analyst profession and helps BAs become better communicators, learn new technical skills, and find fulfilling careers in business analysis.

Prior to founding *Bridging the Gap* and *My Business Analysis Career,* Laura held a variety of information technology roles and has been instrumental in establishing business analyst practices in several organizations.

Table of Contents

Preface

Why did I choose to write this book?

I believe we each have a passion, a career we were meant to do and within which we will find fulfillment. We might have several of these, but we all have at least one. Each of us has a responsibility to pursue this passion and to stay on a path toward finding real fulfillment in our work. And once we find the right fit, we owe it to ourselves to do regular gut checks to know if this is "the career" or just a step toward "the career". My thinking here is heavily influenced by Po Bronson's *What Should I do with my Life?*[1] This is an amazing book full of stories of real-life people just like you and I who have struggled with this question.

I believe that I have found my passion in the set of activities involved in being a business analyst. I fully believe that my job title will change several times before I die (or decide to retire). I might even decide that I want to bridge a different gap—i.e., foregoing the business and IT gap for any other set of disparate people or building different types of systems. Regardless, the core of what I love about this profession will remain unchanged for me personally. To be completely forthright, I am still trying to figure out my BA flavor...why I really love this profession

---

[1] *What Should I Do with my Life?: The True Story of People Who Answered the Ultimate Question,* by Po Bronson. 2005.

and what I can do to ensure I pick more of the right projects to work on that will keep this fun for me. But my gut says I am pretty darn close. Still searching, always open to fresh ideas, but I am close.

I have chosen to write this book with the hope of helping other talented professionals discover if business analysis is their passion and, if so, help them on their journey into the profession.

Thank you for purchasing this book and allowing me to help you on your journey.

ACKNOWLEDGEMENTS

Writing a book like this would not have been possible without the professional support of my fellow business analysts, those I have met personally here in Denver and those with whom I collaborate via online communities.

Special thanks go to those who agreed to be interviewed—you'll find their ideas, inspirational stories, and advice throughout the book:

- Jonathan Babcock, www.practicalanalyst.com, @jonbab1, with extra thanks for the many citations, up-to-date links and practical recommendations he provided outside the interview, as well as detailed feedback on the content which helped make this a clearer text.
- Doug Goldberg, @DougGtheBA, with special thanks for detailed feedback of the content and

pointing out some missing sections. His feedback helped make this a better resource overall.

- Megan Herlily
- Ted Hellmuth, Division Director of Robert Half Technology
- Doug Hill, @dougiemac
- Lori Lister
- David Wright, @dwwright99

I also want to thank Ellen Gottesdiener for reviewing an early version of the book and providing feedback. Finally, I owe many thanks to members of my Twitter and blog communities who were always ripe with fresh resources and ideas, many of which were incorporated directly into this book.

And never did I feel alone on this journey, but always supported by my husband, David Brandenburg, my parents, Michael and Terry Brandau, and my dear friend, Heather Peck, who helped me find the courage to pursue my goal of publishing a book. They all had confidence in me every step of the way and for that I will always be grateful.

Business Analyst Manifesto

Out of chaos, we create order.

Out of disagreement, we create alignment.

Out of ambiguity, we create clarity.

But most of all, we create positive change for the organizations we serve.

Business analysts lead teams from the inside out. We create positive change for our organizations. We inspire others to follow us on our path toward positive change. We help everyone understand exactly what that change is and how they can contribute to it. We help teams discover what the change should be.

Ask yourself, are you focused on:

- Leading a team toward the best possible solution to the problem we've been tasked with solving?
- Leading a team to balance our goals with our constraints to achieve a valuable result?
- Developing a shared understanding of what needs to be accomplished?
- Helping the business own the solution?

On every successful project you'll find a business analyst. Their title might be director of technology, product owner, product manager, requirements analyst, business process engineer, VP of operations, development lead, team lead, project manager, or CTO. The title is rather irrelevant. The activities of creating alignment around a clear understanding of "done" that creates positive change is what it means to be a business analyst.

Not everyone with the title "business analyst" holds themselves to these principles. Many people who consider themselves part of our profession are more focused on documents, activities, and sign-offs, than clarity and alignment. They are more focused on filling a specific set of responsibilities than defining a role that helps drive change in their organization. Some are even more focused on getting by day-to-day than on continuous improvement of their abilities.

It will take an inter-connected group of self-motivated people doing excellent business analysis to build a great profession.

We build our profession one BA at a time.

Let us go forward together and discover what it is to do <u>business analysis at its best</u>. Let us come together as professionals who care about doing our best work and help each other take more confident steps forward.

Introduction

Who should read this book?

This book is written for people who are either exploring the possibility of business analysis as a future career or who have decided business analysis is the right career choice but would like some help making the transition.

This book is geared toward business analysts in the information technology space. In this sense, "business analyst" is used to identify individuals who facilitate requirements and organizational changes as part of delivering software solutions.

One core assumption behind the book is that business analysis is a profession that values career experience. It is relatively rare to find even entry-level business analyst positions that do not require some level of professional experience. This is because the role relies heavily on prior knowledge of how organizations work that is best gained through other entry-level positions.

If you are a recent college grad, this book will not likely help you land a business analyst position in the next few months, but it will help you shape your short-term decisions to accumulate the experience required to qualify yourself for an entry-level business analyst position within a few years.

There are plenty of books out there that offer an overview of the fundamentals of business analysis.

This book does not try to replace those, but instead augments those books by helping you sort through what you need to learn, do, and achieve to find your first business analyst position.

A note about recommended resources

That being said, this book is not the only resource you'll need to learn about being a business analyst. This book is chock full of references to additional resources, some free online resources and some cost-effective books. You'll notice that many of the books seem dated, but that does not make them irrelevant. Some of the best books about the fundamentals are 5-10 years old.

I recommend books because you can read a chapter or two, find a way to apply what you learned, and move at a self-directed pace that is comfortable to you. If you find learning through books difficult or just want the accountability of a more structured approach, consider finding a mentor or a coach. If you are going to invest money in formal training without much experience to make that training "stick", you'll do a lot better to spread that training time over several months than to try to learn everything you need to know about business analysis in a couple of days. One-on-one coaching provides that sort of flexibility and the training can grow as you grow professionally and adjust to support changes in your situation.

Originally, I did not recommend any training programs because formal training is way too expensive and situational for me to venture a meaningful recommendation without knowing a lot more about your personal situation. Also, throughout my research, I found very little evidence that professionals without BA experience benefited from formal training before finding their first position. Training is the most beneficial when you can apply it immediately in your day-to-day work. It can also be beneficial if you have previous experiences doing BA-type activities and want to solidify those experiences into a formal model.

However, after speaking with many past purchasers through my Career Mentoring program, I realized there are situations where the potential business analyst benefits from training. I've since updated this text to reference cost-effective programs in specific situations.

Getting the most out of this book

The chapters and sections are organized in a logical progression starting with deciding on a business analyst career, then learning about the profession and building experiences, then finding a job. You can choose to jump around or jump ahead. For the most part each section is relatively discrete and valuable on its own. While the "Putting it to Practice" exercises do sometimes assume you've completed the earlier tasks, it should be relatively simple for you to pick these up in the middle or back track just enough to complete the task at hand.

Regardless of where you start or the path you choose to take through this book, with each step you will be more informed, better prepared, and armed full of tips and techniques to help you make this journey. You will benefit from leveraging my personal experience accumulated by finding my way into the profession and hiring many people into business analyst positions, and also the experience of those who contributed their time and knowledge to be interviewed for this book. As you make your way through the text, be inspired by their stories. Not so long ago, we all sat where you are right now: pondering our next career move, trying to make a difference, and wondering how to get there from here.

I am a firm believer in self-discovery. This book is a guide to developing a self-directed plan for starting a business analyst career. Each section contains "Putting it to Practice" exercises which help you act on what you learn in each chapter. This is not a book to read passively and simply hope that the perfect job lands in your lap. You will benefit the most if you take the time to do a fair amount of the exercises involving, thinking, writing, self-assessment, self-reflection, and research. I can give you the tools you need to find success. It is up to you to use those tools. This said some of the exercises simply might not resonate with you. Spend the most time where you feel like you are learning the most.

You also might want to share your experiences or ask follow-up questions. I've started a LinkedIn group specifically for potential business analysts and experienced business analysts who want to help potential business analysts enter the profession: Start a Business Analyst Career. Please join us. Help others and find the additional help you need as you make your way through this book.

To get started find a notebook or start a file folder on your computer dedicated to your thoughts on this career change and what you collect as you continue your research. You might want to initiate this new notebook by jotting down some thoughts about what you hope to achieve through this career change journey.

Putting it to Practice # 1

Take the BA Litmus Test

This exercise will help you explore business analysis as a career choice and evaluate whether or not you could pursue this profession as a passion. You can take this test any way you like. I suggest writing a few sentences or a few paragraphs in response to each question in your new notebook or computer folder.

1. Do you find yourself in meetings very often? If so, do you like them? What do you like about the meetings you do attend? If you don't like them, why?
2. How do you deal with situations where people are clearly not communicating? Do you naturally find yourself paraphrasing others in order to help them communicate?
3. Do you like to write? Is your writing precise and clear?

4. Are you comfortable working independently at your desk/computer for 2-3 hours at a time?
5. When you use a new tool or website, are you content with how it works or do you think of ways to make it better?
6. In situations of conflict, do you find you can maintain a neutral or at least balanced position and see both sides of the argument?
7. Are you comfortable drawing on a white board? Do you get excited about seeing people align around a concept or idea?
8. Do you find yourself intuitively understanding new systems and dissecting the rules that make them work? Are you driven to understand why things work the way they do?
9. Would you say you have a good understanding of the organizations of which you have been a part? Do you know who is responsible for what and how things are accomplished? (Examples could include a community organization, educational institution, club, or company.)
10. Do you tend to enjoy starting projects more than finishing them? (As a BA, the bulk of your effort goes into initiating a project. Of course, you must be willing to finish off your deliverables.)
11. Do you like to ask questions? Do you seem to have a way to ask the right question at the right time?
12. Do people at work tend to confide in you? Do people at work tend to come to you to help them think through a problem or make a decision?

13. Do you like to solve problems? Especially the really tough ones? Do you see these as opportunities to strut your mental prowess and not as annoyances?
14. Do you enjoy learning? Do you tend to pick up new skills and techniques quickly?
15. Do you like to support collaboration among the people you work with? Do you tend to get more people involved in problems and solutions instead of less?

If you can answer yes to most of the above questions, it's likely that business analysis might be a possible career for you to find your passion. It's not a guarantee; this isn't a scientific test. But it is based on my personal experience, what I love about the role, and my interviews with other business analysts who really "get it" and are happy with their career choice.

If you can't answer yes to most of these questions, this may not the right career choice. But it also might mean that you lack some of the prerequisite professional experience to really know for sure. Continue reading forward a few more chapters to explore the profession in more depth.

If you are not sure just continue reading and be ready to explore. We're nowhere near done yet.

Chapter 1

What is it like to be a business analyst?

This chapter is intended to help you see yourself in a business analyst's shoes. Decisions become easier if we can see and feel what the end result will be like. I invite you to absorb what's written here and see yourself in various aspects of the role. You will also have the opportunity to do more exploration in this area when you talk to business analysts, as suggested in a later chapter.

TYPICAL DAY

What typical day? There is no typical day as a business analyst. Rather, there are multiple different kinds of days, some of which tend to repeat themselves throughout project lifecycles and some of which bear no explanation.

Business analysis is not the type of career where you need to necessarily be prepared for anything, but expect the occasional surprise or unexpected situation. In most business analyst jobs, you'll experience a fair amount of variety in your day-to-day work. And while this is not a role like IT support requiring near constant interaction with others and real-time prioritization, priorities shift and a certain amount of flexibility and responsiveness is important. Of course, if your company experiences a catastrophe or uncovers significant unexpected opportunity you will most likely be called in to help on short notice, but that's the exception not the rule.

Most often your days will not hit you, instead you'll hit them. The best business analysts drive the requirements process. This means scheduling meetings, managing input, influencing stakeholders, and ensuring decisions are made. Great business analysts are proactive and seek out answers. If this is not a comfortable role for you, it might be possible to find positions where you can partner with a strong project manager. In general, however, you should be prepared for planning out your own work to meet deadlines (possibly set by yourself, possibly imposed) and facilitating input and occasionally follow-ups from a variety of people to achieve your end goals.

While there is not one typical day, there are several kinds of typical days.

During project initiation
Project initiation mainly involves eliciting requirements to understand the scope of a potential solution. Elicitation days are fun and many business analysts enjoy elicitation days the most. These days occur early in the project or possibly even before the project starts and involve meeting with stakeholders to understand what they want to achieve in a project. You will spend the day drinking from a fire hose because you will be learning so much and handling so many different perspectives about the project. You'll often spend the afternoon or evening typing up your copious notes and analyzing what you learned. I find elicitation to be a very intellectual activity. All of your intellectual capabilities and strengths are stretched to the max as you help creative and idea-laden people

identify, sort, and crystallize their best ideas into concrete proposals scoping a tangible project.

After your initial interviews or facilitation sessions, you'll have days where you are pulling together what you learned and creating readable, consumable documents identifying scope. These days may be filled with follow-up questions, emails, phone calls, or impromptu meetings. You'll be creating visuals and textual documents and facilitating review sessions.

> *Business analysts excel at dealing with ambiguity and helping create clarity.*

During elicitation, business analysts handle ambiguity and create clarity. This phase may involve rooting out opposing opinions among stakeholders and surfacing these issues. This time is full of dialog, thinking, and communication. You draw; you write; you vet; you review. You think "I've got it" only to find new flaws. You back track a bit, reset, and continue pressing forward. At times, the ambiguity might seem a bit overwhelming.

In the early days in a new company you might also be acquiring basic knowledge about the system, product, and organization. You'll also be meeting new people and learning how they work and communicate. You'll often feel like the *least* knowledgeable person in the room. But that's OK because it's your role to facilitate, not necessarily have all the answers.

During requirements elaboration

Once you've defined the project scope, your days may take on a more syncopated pace. You'll be working from a requirements management plan (whether written or not, by this time you'll have a plan of sorts) and exploring specific sections of the overall scope in more detail, creating visuals, requirements documents, and reviewing them with your team. These days tend to break up into about one-third meetings and two-thirds independent work. As a new business analyst, you might start a project at this phase under the wing of a senior business analyst or project manager.

In most organizations, the bulk of time is spent in elaboration. These activities are often likened to peeling the layers of an onion as you progressively dive into deeper details and strengthen the alignment around the solution. From elicitation to elaboration, a shift from ambiguity to relative certainty occurs. Not to say that elaboration is a purely logical progression. You will encounter problems, unknowns, unexpected cases, and there are a variety of interesting problems to solve. You might still feel like you are drinking from a fire hose from time to time. One need uncovers another and so on and so forth.

As the issues become smaller and the risk of drastic change is minimized, you will begin to review the requirements with the implementation team to get their input on the direction and the overall solution. Many organizations use document reviews or walk-throughs to ensure the entire team understands the requirements and can implement them. The final requirements specifications need to blend what the business wants with what can be accomplished given the project and system constraints. During this time you will be helping negotiate trade-offs and often solving technical problems. Some requirements are fairly simple to implement. Others create challenges and involve multiple iterations where you clarify the business need, delve into the details of possible solution, go back to the business with ideas, and so on and so forth until you obtain consensus on a go-forward plan.

This phase is all about thinking or facilitating groups around thinking (not to be confused with "group think"). This involves putting something out for review, getting feedback, making modifications. Repeat. Repeat. Repeat.

As developers design the system, you'll be involved in discussions or formal reviews, ensuring that the business requirements are fulfilled. In some organizations, there are formal traceability practices in place and you could be involved in mapping requirements to design or test documentation to ensure the requirements are covered completely

During project implementation

Once implementation begins, the business analyst (unless they are also filling the role of project manager) is no longer driving the process and the project will most likely implement while you are starting in on something else. You will be responding to questions from developers and testers as well as resolving issues about the requirements as they come up. Depending on the organization's methodology, you might also be keeping documentation in sync with how the final product works. Depending on the role and other roles within the company, you may help train the business users, creating help documentation, identifying and implementing new business processes, or helping assure the delivered product for quality. But none of these previous activities necessarily will be the responsibility of the business analyst in a given organization.

During implementation, projects can hit a snag and the BA might be brought in to lead the team through solving a difficult problem or rethinking a requirement. This often means an impromptu meeting to identify potential solutions to a difficult-to-address requirement or unexpected dependency within the system. Especially under deadlines, these discussions can become heated and you might find yourself right in the middle of it.

It's important that you are psychologically prepared to leave your project before it's done. The first major project I worked on, after having spent the better part of 4-5 months conceptualizing the product and detailing out requirements, was released while I was on the opposite side of the country on vacation and with limited web connectivity. Many BAs speak to having trouble finishing things. We tend to be starters, not finishers.

But then again...it's different in an agile environment

All of the above is true in a traditional environment. In agile environments many IT roles change. Given how this trend is gaining increasing acceptance it is very likely you will be working within an agile environment at some point in your career. The BA role in agile is fairly ill-defined. There are portions of the product owner role that are clearly business analysis activities. Oftentimes the business analyst either fills the product owner role or directly supports the product owner.

If you find a position in an agile shop, it's safe to hypothesize you'll be doing the above sorts of activities but in smaller increments and all within the span of 2-4 weeks. Your days actually might be more "typical" from one week to the next as you balance all these activities to deliver just-in-time requirements.

FREQUENTLY ASKED QUESTIONS

How will I be managed?

You will typically have a project manager or functional manager overseeing your work. Business analysts are not typically micro-managed. Because the role requires your best thinking and a great deal of in depth analysis, you might be the only one who really sees the whole picture of what needs to be accomplished and how you intend to get there. Even though you've got it straight in your head, expect to externalize that plan for the benefit of others who you will need involved as well as those, like the project managers, who will track your progress.

What motivates a business analyst?

Most business analysts are self-motivated people with high standards for quality and completeness. Given that we are typically working well-ahead of project delivery, it is necessary to stay on top of priorities for deadlines that are weeks if not months away. Analysis activities almost always take longer than anticipated as unexpected issues come up. Staying ahead of the game ensures you stay on track.

How will I get feedback on my work?

You will likely receive a lot of feedback on your deliverables, not necessarily you personally. As a business analyst you are constantly publishing documents, visuals and interpretations to your

> *"As a business analyst, you have to be willing to make mistakes and learn from them, especially in the beginning."*
>
> **-Megan Herlily   Business Analyst**

stakeholders and teammates for critique. Be prepared to get their honest feedback. Welcome it. This is part of the requirements process. Many business analysts are perfectionists by nature and this can make it difficult to watch people point out your "mistakes" in a meeting or an email. The key is to separate yourself from your deliverables. Let your deliverables take the beating. It will make them better.

Will I be able to telecommute?

Business analysis is a mixed bag when it comes to telecommuting. If you plan to work locally and full-time, expect to be in the office at least 3-4 days per week. In-person communication is just too important for this role and to try to do things over the phone when you could just as easily be in the office is unnecessary. However, working one day a week from home can help you set aside time for analysis and documentation and it's often a good approach, provided the company you will be working for supports it.

Even with a local office, so many companies have offices across the country (and multiple countries) today that you might be on the phone anyway or you might be traveling to meet with your stakeholders.

What's it like to work with remote offices?

Working with remote offices changes the role significantly. It is more difficult to build relationships and communicate over the phone and through email. You need more patience and more tech savvy (to run online meetings and potentially update documents in real-time) and particularly strong communication skills. I know a lot of great BAs who struggle when asked to deal primarily with remote stakeholders and don't enjoy the job as much.

Will I be required to travel?

There is no standard amount of travel time for a BA position. If you find a position with a consulting company you could travel every week, potentially to different clients. If you find a position with a local company, you may never leave your city. But with the plethora of companies having multiple offices, it's likely that a BA position will require occasional travel, either to elicit requirements from stakeholders in a remote office or to kick-off a project with an out-sourced technology team.

In what locations will I find BA jobs?

The majority of BA jobs are going to be found in your larger cities and most will be onsite. As mentioned before, the BA role is not a good candidate for telecommuting, unless the whole office is virtual (and that's a different book entirely). Consider the technology and corporate market in your area. If there are decent-sized businesses that make significant investments in technology each year, there are probably some BA (or BA-like) positions. But if not, then you may need to consider relocating to a more tech-heavy market.

Inter-personal interaction

During my career discovery journey through the PathFinder ™, I found that a balance approximately one-third interacting with others and two-thirds working independently was ideally suited to my personality and communication style. I discovered when I had more independent time I was soon bored and lacked motivation but if my responsibilities required I spend much more than three-fifths of time interacting with others I became tired and distracted from all the extroversion.

It's quite possible that each individual can slightly tip the BA role to meet their personal balance, but if you think you'd like to spend more than 50% of your time interacting with others this is probably not the career choice for you. With that much interaction, you simply won't have the time to do the documentation and analysis that makes individuals in this role successful.

What types of companies hire BAs?

In general BAs are hired by larger companies that are investing in software application development and large software purchases. They might be developing a software product or service (such as QuickBooks or an online job board) or creating software for internal use (for example, a system to manage an internal publishing process). Other companies that hire BAs are consulting companies that complete projects for the types of companies above. Consulting companies might serve the shorter-term technology needs of a smaller company or take on a project within a larger software development portfolio in a larger company.

What types of projects will I work on?

All kinds of software projects can benefit from the contributions of a business analyst. I've never worked on two projects that were the same. Some projects focus on customizing off-the-shelf tools that are purchased. Some projects involve completely custom software development – i.e., they are built from scratch. Others are a combination of the two and this is becoming an increasing trend as there are an increasing number of tools to purchase or rent. Others projects iterate on an existing platform. These projects essentially customize the platform to answer a new business problem.

Will I ever be bored?

Maybe. No job is 100% exciting and business analysis has its share of mundane activities such as copious meeting notes, maintaining documentation like issues logs, conducting last pass document review meetings, finalizing the impact of seemingly insignificant changes throughout a web of documentation, and at times documenting what already exists so it can be evaluated and possibly rebuilt. But the mundane details are tied to a goal – high product quality – and measured by successful teams and the lack of overlooked details in the 11th hour.

Will I make decisions?

Good business analysts tend to be quiet leaders. As a business analyst, you will not typically have direct authority over others or make the big decisions on your own, but you will have a lion's share of influence if you choose to exert it. In general, business analysts facilitate and create collaboration to drive the decision-making process more often than they get to make the big decisions.

With whom will I work?

You will work with a wide variety of people from throughout the different departments and different levels of the organization. In a small-to-mid-sized company (and even as a new business analyst) you might have some executive exposure, especially if an executive is the sponsor for your project. You will be balancing executive perspectives with those of the people who work with the system day-to-day. You can expect to have contact with people in a variety of office positions who are not very familiar with technology and what it can do to help them. You will be interviewing these future users and possibly even shadowing them to understand how they do their job and help find ways that technology might solve business problems. If you are working for a company where software is the product, you will likely have a primary contact within marketing or product management. In this scenario, the owner within product or marketing is responsible for the vision of what is to be built and the business analyst works with them to articulate that vision and detail the solution.

On the flip side, you will be working with colleagues across the technology group, primarily project managers, developers, and quality assurance engineers. If the project emphasizes UI design, you might also collaborate with a user experience professional or user interface designer to maintain consistency between the design and the requirements. If the project involves large amounts of content you will likely work with editors, content managers, corporate librarians, or other information professionals to align requirements with content organization and structure. As you move from entry-level to enterprise-level, you will also work with architects and leaders within the IT department to scope and plan projects or align business needs with the IT direction.

Will I work more with the business or with the technology team?

It depends. If you start the project with a well-defined idea and your efforts are focused on working through the details, you might work with a handful of business stakeholders and very closely with the implementation team on the functional requirements. Alternatively, there might be a fair amount of exploration to be done before the idea can even crystallize. In these cases you start further within the business by exploring the business processes and opportunities.

Depending on how the role is defined within your organization, you might take the project requirements to the last detail in each screen or you might "finish" the project with a high-level flow and set of features and someone else might work through the details. Some organizations split the role into two by employing a business analyst who focuses more on the business side of the process and delivers business requirements and a systems or requirements analyst who fleshes out the business requirements into functional specifications within a system or set of systems.

Will I have work-life balance?

Few people like to bring their job home. As far as career choices go, especially within technology, a full-time BA position with a local company is probably one that least infringes on home life. (This answer is going to be very different for independent consultants or individuals working as business analysts for a consulting company.) Because the bulk of your work is in the upfront stages of a project, your activities tend not to be quite as deadline driven. (There are many exceptions to this. I've also started on projects where the development team is ready to start 2-4 weeks down the road. This creates a lot of short-term pressure to get the scope right and get some details defined until you can get ahead of the development team.)

What you are more likely to bring "home" with you is a problem that you have not solved or a communication issue you want to improve on. The circumstances of the business analysis role, when you really care about it, can consume your at-home thinking. The BA role typically does not require hefty amounts of over-time or off-hours work, though of course it's always possible given the company culture and project expectations.

How will my work be defined?
Business analysts are typically given a fair amount of freedom in their work and how they accomplish their objectives. In an organization with a formal software development process, the outputs of your work may be fairly well defined and you may need to strictly adhere to some established templates and frameworks. There might also be formal gates that each project goes through and a BA will have a critical role in bringing a project through the initial gates. In an organization with less formality or in a situation where you are the first BA within an organization you might have the opportunity to create the requirements process.

Who will I report to?
In a matrix organization you will have both a project manager to report to for project-specific deliverables and a functional manager, who will oversee the overall process and your work as a business analyst. In some organizations, the project manager is also the BA's supervisor.

Once I master the basics, will it continue to be a challenge?

The business analyst role involves one challenge after another. If you are not trying to identify a new business problem, then you are wrestling with a new communication situation.   You'll often have opportunities to stay abreast of technology trends and experiment with new tools and techniques. But as roles are blending more and more, understanding new applications for technology is becoming of increasing importance.

> *"I like the fact that BA work does not change as fast as software development but that I am continuously learning."*
>
> *-Doug Goldberg, Sr. Business Analyst*

What's not going to change all that much are the fundamentals of business analysis. If you focus on learning the fundamentals and work your way through a few projects, you will reach a point where you have mastered the basic techniques but can continue refining the art. There is no one "best way" to do business analysis and there is no "typical situation", so you will always be able to learn something new that might help you tomorrow, even as the underlying fundamentals remain consistent.

Is business analysis a competitive profession?

Being a business analyst is definitely cooperative within the context of your organization though there may be some opportunities to be competitive with respect to other organizations. Your main focus is helping align a set of diverse people to a single goal. If you are an overly competitive person, this could get in the way of attaining the end goal.

The measures of your success as a BA can be hard to nail down. Sure that project was what your stakeholder really wanted but what exactly was your role in that? If someone else had applied a different set of techniques would things have come out the same or different? Better or worse? You will need to be secure in yourself, consistently do the best job you can, and give yourself some self-recognition when you cool that heated debate or ask just the right question to get just the right answer. If you are doing your job, oftentimes everyone else will be too busy thinking to notice your role.

How difficult will it be to find a job?

If you are truly passionate about the role and most responsibilities required by the role come naturally to you, it should not be any more difficult to find a BA job than to find a job in most other professional positions. In some respects, the barriers to entry are lower than other IT jobs because as of yet there are no expectations for formal training or specific technical knowledge. The technical skills of a business analyst are relatively easy to learn, but might take a lifetime to perfect. There is no one stamp of approval that makes you a great business analyst, so you might spend some time gathering relevant experiences and learning the techniques.

On the other hand, many business analyst positions are looking for individuals with experience. Because there is no single path into the profession or degree to get and therefore qualify yourself for a position, it can be challenging to carve a path into your first position. Creating situations where you can get the necessary experiences or finding someone who recognizes your talents in lieu of your experience is the challenge.

On a related note, business analysis skills will remain relatively timeless. While software development skills become quickly out-dated, what makes a good business analyst is not changing quite so quickly. This makes it a great profession for people looking to try out multiple careers or leave the professional world for a period of time to raise children or pursue other interests.

What impact will I have?

Just like most professions, business analysts can work in non-profit and other good-doing organizations, but as a profession, business analysis is not geared toward specifically doing good works. Your requirements could have an adverse impact on society or a positive one, it really depends on the vision of your stakeholder.   Of course, as an independent professional you choose who you work for and what kind of work you do.

The impact a business analyst makes is most keenly felt within the organization or by its customers. As a representative of the organization's diverse set of individuals who use software everyday to accomplish their objectives, your mission to make the software better can help make their work-days more productive and efficient. It can automate repetitive tasks and allow individuals to focus on more complex tasks. Or, quite honestly, the software you help design could put people out of a job.

"A strong desire to help others....is a very strong driver for deep facilitation, effective elicitation, relationship building, and mentoring."

-Doug Goldberg, Business Analyst

Sometimes business analysts are being brought into organizations where the role did not exist before. In these situations, you have a huge opportunity to make an impact on the work lives of the technical team. Recent studies suggest poor requirements practices account for many project failures.[2] Set cost savings aside and consider the lives of individuals on these teams as they worked day by day on a project headed toward failure, trying to write code for unclear or non-existent requirements, participating in heated discussions with no resolution, and time spent working on features that never saw the light of day. Business analysts insert themselves in the thick of these situations and, in my personal opinion, have a positive impact on the relationships between project team members. This is part of what personally keeps me going when I am working through some of the more mundane details involved with the role.

Putting it to Practice # 2

What excites you about being a BA? What are your areas of concern?

It's time to get that notebook back out. Go through the above details about the role and list a few that energized you. Write a few sentences, or paragraphs if you are inspired, about what that experience means to you. What made you excited about becoming a business analyst? How will you feel doing these activities? What will be fun? What more do you want to know about this part of the job?

---

[2] For example, Keith Ellis claims more than 41% of development resources are consumed on unnecessary or poorly specified requirements. Business Analysis Benchmark Study, *The Impact of Business Requirements on the Success of Technology Projects*, IAG Consulting, 2008.

Now go back through the items that made you ponder or possibly even doubt your decision. Write as precisely as you can why these aspects made you nervous. Do you feel you would dislike some aspect of that task? Do you lack the confidence that you could do it? It's important not to let your doubts become barriers. It may just be that you need to learn a bit more or have a few trial runs to discover what this part of the job is really like.

As you go through this exercise, you will probably start to have some questions. Start a list of your questions somewhere in your notebook. We will use them in a later chapter.

Putting it to Practice # 3

Start looking at business analyst job descriptions
As you are considering entering a new profession, one of the most beneficial things you can do is to start developing habits that promote continuous learning. One habit I've found particularly beneficial is to stay aware of the language used in job postings. Spend some time each week reviewing the business analyst postings on various job boards. Print or save the ones that seem the most relevant to you or have a unique aspect that interests you.

As you develop this habit, begin looking beyond business analyst positions and to other related positions that incorporate business analyst responsibilities. As you incorporate this habit of learning into your weekly routine, you'll be amazed at how your awareness of positions, jobs, and roles increases,

If you need help finding job boards to search, look ahead to the section on "Using job boards" in Chapter 7.

Chapter 2

What do I need to know about business analysis?

Before you dive into this section, get out pens or highlighters of at least two different colors. If you are reading online you can use the online editing functionality of your reader or simply have ready a sheet of paper with room for three lists.

As you read this section be aware of areas in which you believe you have a good understanding. Consider "good understanding" to mean if you needed to do it tomorrow you probably could pull it off, possibly with a brief refresher. Secondly be aware of things that confuse you or that you don't understand much at all, i.e. you don't feel like you could do them tomorrow.

We'll use this information later to help you craft a plan from where you are at in terms of your BA experiences to where you want to be: a prepared, confident potential business analyst.

BUSINESS ANALYSIS DEFINED

According to IIBA:

> *"A business analyst works as a liaison among stakeholders in order to elicit, analyze, communicate and validate requirements for changes to business processes, policies and information systems. The business analyst understands business problems and opportunities in the context of the*

requirements and recommends solutions that enable the organization to achieve its goals."[3]

In essence, the business analyst helps the team move from ambiguity about the goals and scope to clarity. Regardless of the processes used, moving from ambiguity to clarity is an iterative process. Sometimes it's like peeling an onion, layer by layer, but other times the route can be more complex and the road less focused. These activities can be applied to all kinds of "changes" from organization-wide strategies to specific projects or initiatives.

As a new or junior business analyst, you will most likely be working on one or more specific projects that someone else (whether your manager or a project manager or an executive) will have put some basic scope around. As you become more experienced, you will be able to leverage your BA experiences to get involved in the upfront work in defining project concepts or helping to drive new strategies and programs. The rest of this section is written from the perspective of working on a relatively finite project as that is what your first business analysis experiences will likely involve.

We will start by taking each of the core responsibilities "elicit, analyze, communicate and validate requirements" and break them down into some reasonable expectations. Then we will look at

---

[3]http://www.theiiba.org/AM/Template.cfm?Section=Becoming_a_BA&Template=/CM/HTMLDisplay.cfm&ContentID=4377

some broader knowledge areas that business analysts need to know about, including specific tools, technical skills and software development lifecycles.

ELICITATION

Elicitation is the process of working with stakeholders to understand what they want to achieve through the project or change effort. A project stakeholder is someone who owns or provides input on a specific aspect of a project. Stakeholders might have a very clear picture of what they want or they might be vague or ambiguous. Some stakeholders are clear on the vision, but fuzzy on the details. Others think clearly about the details but lose track of the big picture. Elicitation involves bringing out the best thoughts and ideas about the change from all the stakeholders.

The *Business Analysis Body of Knowledge (BABOK®)* lists the following techniques for eliciting requirements.

- Brainstorming
- Document Analysis
- Focus group
- Interface analysis
- Interviews
- Observation
- Prototyping
- Requirements work-shops

- Survey/questionnaires[4]

By far the most common technique used is a variation of the interview, whether one-on-one or in a group interview session. Because interviews are a common technique to address many different business problems you have probably done an interview somewhere in your previous work.

Interviews involve thoughtful questioning and active listening. As a BA, you want to internalize as much of what the others have to say as possible. During

> *You can rarely go wrong by clarifying the problem to be solved before discussing how to solve it.*

elicitation it is less important that you fully analyze what you hear than that you actually comprehend it, have the tools in place to remember the salient points (most likely by taking notes) and can follow-up with the analysis at a later time.

During elicitation you will typically work with a variety of stakeholders from all levels of the organization. Stakeholders can include:

---

[4] *A Guide to the Business Analysis Body of Knowledge (BABOK® Guide).* International Institute of Business Analysis. 2009. Page 53.

- **Business Owners** of the system or project from a business perspective, often at the executive level.
- **Users** of the new system or process, often called **subject matter experts**.
- **Product managers** or other **"user proxies"** who represent the end user or customer of the system.
- **Technical or Enterprise Architects** and other technical stakeholders who are responsible for overseeing the overall IT strategy.

Key skills for elicitation include:

- **Organizing meetings**: Inviting the right people, setting a meeting goal, crafting an agenda, and documenting and distributing meeting notes.
- **Facilitating discussions**: Ability to facilitate a meeting by initiating discussions and keeping the dialog moving and focused on the topic at hand. The best meeting facilitators keep track of the discussion, elicit input from everyone, redirect conversation around overly forceful personalities or off-topic comments, and drive follow up on open points in the discussion.
- **Planning**. As you "peel the onion" you will be progressing toward a defined system. Part of elicitation involves having a plan to get from nothing to something.
- **Conducting walk-throughs and demos**: Elicitation involves obtaining feedback on concepts, rules, and deliverables. This activity

might involve a document walk-through or a demo of a wireframe or prototype.

- **Asking good questions**. Ability to get to the heart of the matter and ask a question that drives deeper understanding of the problem or solution space.
- **Relationship Building**. Elicitation requires trust and foundational to trust is building relationships with your stakeholders. They need to trust that you are on their side and will do what you can to help them see their ideas through to fruition.

Although elicitation will be one of the first BA activities on a project, it does not end with the initial requirements elicitation activities. You will come back to elicitation throughout the requirements lifecycle as you help the team achieve a clearer picture of what the change entails.

ANALYSIS AND SPECIFICATION

As the business analyst makes his or her way from the initial scoping of the change to the details of the change, the requirements process becomes driven more by analysis than elicitation—i.e., we are refining ideas more than we are generating new ones. Wikipedia defines analysis as "the process of breaking a complex topic or substance into smaller parts to gain a better understanding of it. ...".5 A business

---

5 http://en.wikipedia.org/wiki/Analysis. Accessed 5/13/2009.

analyst analyzes the input of stakeholders with the goal of creating a comprehensive understanding of the "changes to business processes, policies, and information systems."

Analysis is the process of solving the actual problem, in terms of specifying requirements, creating visuals that represent the new process or software

> *"The biggest learning curve for a new business analyst is what a good tech spec would look like to a developer. Ask them 'What would good documentation look like? What do good requirements look like?'"*
>
> *-Ted Hellmuth, IT Recruiter, Division Director, Robert Half Technology*

application, and developing work-flows and business processes. Requirements specifications are the result of detailed analysis about a set of requirements. Some deliverable templates heavily support the analysis process by encouraging thinking about flows, rules, exceptions, and boundaries. Often in breaking down the problem, the business analyst will find inconsistencies between what the stakeholders want and what makes logical sense.

Throughout the analysis process, the business analyst brings stakeholders from both the business and technical side in to help solve the problems at hand. Analysis often involves the bringing together of both perspectives to find solutions to problems or work through how to solve a specific problem given project or system constraints. Within any given organization, an analyst might involve individuals from a variety of technical disciplines to help negotiate appropriate solutions.

As a new business analyst, you will want to be familiar with what each of the following deliverables is and knowledgeable about how you would go about creating it. You will also want to be able to speak to why you might choose to create a specific deliverable and what value each deliverable adds to the requirements process. Entire books are available on most topics, so treat this as a cursory guide and checklist.

Scope statements/ Features List/ Business Requirements

These types of documents are often the result of the initial elicitation activities and define the scope and the justification of a change from the business perspective. They are often not implementable but they are concrete and drive the activities of a project. You can think of scope statements as a roadmap for a project or initiative, clearly defining boundaries around what is to be achieved, what business objective will be fulfilled, and what's not in of scope.

Functional Requirements

A functional requirements document or list details the intended functions of a new software or system. Most often, functional requirements start with "The system shall" or "The ability to" and are often grouped logically by feature. For a multi-month project, a functional requirements document might easily be in excess of 50 pages. These types of documents best support projects using a variation of the waterfall methodology.

Functional requirements are often given attributes to classify them or group them together in meaningful ways. Some common attributes are:

- Priority
- Owner
- Requestor
- Effort
- Risk

Use Cases

Use cases provide an alternative way to capture functional requirements. Use cases are typically textual descriptions of an interaction between one or more actors and one or more systems. They can be (and often are) accompanied by use case diagrams or system interaction diagrams that visually depict the flow between the actor(s) and system(s). Use cases can be written at varying levels of granularity, from a high-level business process describing the flow through multiple systems to a low-level interaction between two systems or the steps to accomplish a specific business task within a single system.

By and large, use cases are one of the most fundamental techniques of business analysis. As a potential business analyst, it's worth spending some time with a book or online resource to learn the ins and outs. Some excellent resources on use cases include:

- Writing Effective Use Cases, by Alistair Cockburn. 2000.
- Use Case Modeling, by Kurt Bittner and Ian Spence. 2003.
- Use Cases: Requirements in Context, 2nd edition, by Daryl Kulak and Eamonn Guiney. 2003.

Product Backlog

The product backlog is the list of features or requirements for delivery in an agile environment. Backlog items are typically expressed in the following syntax 'As a [user], I want to [do something] to [achieve some objective]'. Backlog items might be at varying levels of detail and a distinction is made between epics and stories. Epics are high-level descriptions of functionality that might encompass a few weeks to a few months of development effort, analogous to a feature or a business requirement. Stories tend to be small enough to be achieved in a few days, analogous to a functional requirement. Like functional requirements, product backlog items might also have attributes.

Requirements or Design?

One of the most common requirements-related debates you'll find in IT circles is whether a certain expression about a project is a "requirement" or an aspect of "design". The most basic answer is requirements express "what is wanted" while design expresses "how to build what is wanted". But as you carve your own path through requirements, you'll discover many expressions that fall in gray areas.

As a new BA it will be easy to fall into traps of allowing business users to tell you how they want the system to be built instead of what it needs to do. Being persistent in asking "why" and clarifying business problems can help uncover many hidden requirements, keeping the requirements specifications focused on what is actually wanted.

User Stories / User Acceptance Tests

User stories are the details behind the product backlog items and how requirements are defined in agile, typically via a set of user acceptance tests. Once the tests pass, the story is considered complete. Consider *User Stories Applied* by Mike Cohn for a summary of what user stories are and how they function as requirements for delivery software in an agile environment. Many teams document user stories on physical index cards that get torn up once obsolete or complete. Others use electronic databases to store this information.

Wireframes / Mock-ups / Prototypes

Nearly everyone you will ask has a different definition of wireframes, mock-ups, and prototypes and this activity is not always part of the business analyst role. In general, wireframes or mock-ups are a collection of documentation or functional code that is used to express the look-and-feel or page layout of an application or website. This can be completed on the infamous "napkin", on a white board, or using a variety of wire-framing tools (see below).

Prototypes tend to be more sophisticated representations of the requirements and might involve working, but skeletal code, or can be built using a simulation tool that allows business logic to be incorporated.

Site Map

A site map will label, organize and define the pages of the website. A site map is especially helpful for a web-based application. A correlating deliverables for an installable software application might be a screen diagram. If you are building new screens or pages, or changing existing screens or pages, a map can help you layout the scope of the application early on and identify gaps in your solution.

Data Models / Data Mapping Specifications

Data models or data mapping specifications communicate core aspects of the requirements in projects data is pushed or pulled between systems. Data models are considered closer to "design" than "requirements" but oftentimes they falls into the business analyst's realm of responsibility. These deliverables represent the data model at a logical level. For example, if you are integrating two systems, you might map data fields at the screen name / label level. (i.e., we want the data element that appears here in system X to appear here in system Y).

The essential characteristic of data models and mapping specifications are that they provide a detailed analysis of how the data flows through the system. The format might be a spreadsheet or a Word document or a diagram. They often include rules for default values, translation rules, allowable values, and optional vs. required values.

Diagrams and UML

Business analysts use diagrams to visually depict process flows, relationships between concepts, or to model systems or project scope. There are a variety of diagrams techniques and new business analysts should minimally be able to create basic work-flow diagrams to visuals a process or a system interaction.

Unified Modeling Language is a specific modeling language used to express the requirements and design of software systems. There are several types of UML diagrams. Most often a BA will be asked to complete domain diagrams, use case diagrams, and occasionally sequence diagrams to accompany a use case. The necessity of UML knowledge will be highly dependent on the particular business analyst position and it is by no means a common job requirement, especially for an entry-level role. You should be generally aware of what it is and how it can be used.

If a job requires or prefers it, you might want to train yourself in a bit more detail prior to an interview. Otherwise, this is a skill to pick up once you have some BA experience. UML diagrams, applied appropriately, can help you guide a team through some of the more gnarly complexities a project faces. I recommend Martin Fowler's *UML Distilled* [6] as a resource for the basics.

User Interface Specifications

User interface specifications detail the rules for a specific screen or page within a system. They help you analyze the rules behind a screen and ensure that all the required functionality has a "home" within the new system. A UI specification may or may not be a BA task, as this is often thought of as an element of design, not requirements, but I've found them tremendously helpful in sorting out potential requirements issues and communicating requirements where the work-flow of the application

---

[6] Martin Fowler, UML Distilled: A Brief Guide to the Standard Object Modeling Language. 2004.

and the look and feel are important to the business stakeholders.

Traceability Matrices

Part of the analysis process is to ensure that every business requirement is fulfilled by a functional requirement and that every functional requirement links back to a business requirement. As you move into deeper details about a project, a traceability matrix helps keep requirements at different levels organized. Some organizations also trace requirements to elements of the design or test cases that validate the requirement was implemented correctly.

Traceability can happen in a formal way using a requirements management tool or in an informal way by doing iterative passes through various documents to make sure everything is covered.

COMMUNICATION

Communication takes many forms for the business analyst. You communicate about the requirements, about the design, and about the issues. You help others communicate amongst themselves to align around a problem or a solution. You communicate verbally, in pictures, and in written documentation.

The business analyst is often responsible first, for helping the stakeholders communicate among themselves about the business problems and opportunities. Most projects have a blend of stakeholders from across the business functions and the business analyst facilitates communication to bring out these alternative perspectives and eventually achieve alignment around project scope.

The business analyst is also responsible for communicating requirements to the implementation team. The end-to-end requirements process involves many individuals, from subject matter experts within the business to implementation engineers (developers, database administrators, IT, QA, user interface designers, etc.). For each deliverable there might be a different set of stakeholders across business and IT involved in creating, reviewing, and approving it. The BA is in the center of all of these groups ensuring that communication about the requirements and the solution is seamless.

Throughout the implementation process, the business analyst will also keep communicating back to the business team. Oftentimes alternatives or constraints surface during implementation and the business analyst needs to bring some possibilities back to the business for a decision.

Written communication

Requirements Specifications
The most prominent form of written communication are the requirements and specification documents you'll create to solidify the requirements. The types of documents are discussed in detail above. When it comes to writing these documents, a business analyst

needs to focus on the clarity of their language. Ambiguous writing or writing that lacks clarity in general will lead to an inefficient requirements process.

Another aspect of written communication is its usability. We typically think of usability in a software context—is this software usable? But this same concept applies to the quality of our documents as well. Usable documents are easier for your business stakeholders and implementation team to consume and therefore understand and provide feedback on the content. Usable documents tend to be well-organized, logical, and consistent. Formatting is one aspect of a usable document, but much more important is how you leverage the format to make the document easy to comprehend.

Finally, consider how large bodies of requirements specifications will be organized for usability and findability. Many organizations use shared file folders for sharing common documents, so the ability to organize several documents in a meaningful folder structure can be useful. Some organizations employ web-based tools with similar folder structures. More formal organizations might employ requirements management tools to manage requirements in a database format. Some progressive teams are using wikis and other collaborative authoring tools to capture requirements. As a business analyst, it's important to think of how to best present information about a project and how to organize that information in a way that will enable people using your documents to find what they are looking for.

Email

As a business analyst you'll also most likely write, read, and respond to a lot of emails. You will probably send emails with documents for review or to coordinate meetings and collaboration. You will receive emails with questions from your stakeholders and developers. Appropriate email communication is a key skill, as is knowing when to pick up the phone or walk down the hall because an email is not an appropriate way to address a particular question.

On some project teams, especially where there is not a great deal of trust, email can become a tool to capture decisions or communicate project constraints. Left unchecked, long email strings can develop as conflicts as issues surface during design or implementation. As a business analyst, you are often in a position to check these unproductive email chains by organizing an impromptu discussion or scheduling a meeting to resolve the issue.

Visual communication

Equally important as written communication is the ability to communicate ideas, concepts, and solutions in a visual way. Visual communication can be very formal such as a UML diagram or other standard modeling notation. It can also be informal, such as drawing on a white board. There are also many middle ground areas such as basic flow charts that look more formal in that they use some notation but are much less complex than a modeling language such as UML.

When using formal forms of visual communication, it's important that you have a good understanding of the formal notation of whatever modeling language you are using. It's equally important that you can abstract that language for your business stakeholders who may not understand that language. The power of visual communication comes when everyone in the room has a shared understanding of what the model presents and so can augment or change it, leveraging the framework for a productive discussion. This might mean you simplify the model for the business or simply that you talk through the key points of the notation so that they are easily understandable. Oftentimes semi-formal models using basic flowchart shapes are much easier to talk through than formal diagrams.

Informal visual communication occurs most often in meetings. Oftentimes someone is trying to express a point of view and verbal communication is simply not adequate. As a business analyst, it can be helpful to draw the conversation as people contribute. This provides a real-time synopsis of where the discussion or problem is at, often including scribbles, around-about lines connecting pieces on two sides of the whiteboard, lists of ideas that need to be kept on hold for the current discussion, etc. This type of communication requires that you be able to carefully listen and abstract what is being said into a shape or a phrase and then visually connect the different concepts as the discussion unfolds. Facilitating this type of communication can also mean taking a step back often enough to ensure it's on track, or encouraging someone else in the room to express their idea by changing the drawing.

Verbal Communication Skills

You'll use your verbal communication skills every day and in every aspect of the project. While it may seem counter-intuitive, the most important verbal communication skill you can develop is your ability to actively listen. Listening involves the act of "hearing" at a most basic level but is really about understanding and asking relevant questions until you develop a shared understanding with the person talking about what is being said. Being a good listener and asking good questions are two trademark skills for a business analyst, but they are not just BA skills. You have opportunities to use and improve on these skills every day, regardless of your profession and employment status.

As a business analyst you might also be called upon to present at a meeting, formal or informal. The ability to speak clearly to groups, coupled with the ability to speak in an organized way can help you excel in a business analyst role. With good public speaking skills, you'll find yourself presenting solutions, taking options to various groups throughout the company, and helping lead product demos or project status reviews.

VALIDATION

Requirements validation involves ensuring the requirements are ready for implementation or ensuring an implemented solution solves the business problem. Validation takes a variety of forms, depending on the formality of the organization. In formal organizations where the requirements are viewed as a contract, validation involves the business formally signing-off on the requirements and the implementation team formally accepting them as buildable. In less formal organizations, validation is part of the natural flow of reviewing deliverables and handing them off for implementation. An agile team might validate in smaller increments and even as part of the actual delivery of the software.

There are some common techniques for validating requirements, though each organization (or project or business analyst) typically customizes these techniques to fit with their set of stakeholders, the scope of the change, and organizational culture.

Structured Walk-Through

A common validation technique involves doing a page-by-page walk-through of the requirements document while encouraging questions and comments to surface potential issues. The reality of our busy office lives is that people are much more likely to actively engage with a document when a walk-through takes place and they hear comments from others than when they review it independently. Also, one comment tends to generate another and everyone benefits from the critical thinking of others in the room.

Structured walk-throughs are most often used when the requirements document needs to be approved or baselined before implementation can begin. They are intended to ensure representatives from business and IT have a common understanding of the project scope. These meetings can often become collaborative as stakeholders across the project team work to understand the requirements and the solution.

Demo

A demo involves showing working software to project stakeholders and subject matter experts to validate that what is built meets their needs. Demos are very powerful because when people see how things will work they can often provide the most valuable feedback. Demos can be the source of requirement clarifications and new requirements.

Using wire-framing tools enables a business analyst to simulate a demo by mocking up potential screens and conducting a walk-through of the look and feel, navigation, and layout of the screens. Simulated demos can provide valuable feedback early in the requirements process and are especially useful in minimizing requirements changes downstream.

Demos are also useful when the solution involves selecting one of several available software packages or services. Demos can be used to compare solutions and the organization might choose to pilot one or more solutions before making a final selection.

Solution assessment

On some projects, the business analyst will be involved in selecting the solution, whether the implementation team is investigating purchasing a commercial off-the-shelf (COTS) product or renting a software-as-a-service (Saas) solution. Choosing to purchase or rent all or part of a solution as opposed to building it custom can have a significant effect on the requirements process. Many of the detailed requirements deliverables discussed as part of the section on analysis will be customized according to the solution selected.

As a business analyst involved in validating a solution, you'll be ensuring the solution meets the business needs. You might perform a gap analysis between the features you've elicited and the capabilities of potential products. The team might take it as far as piloting a few possible solutions, in which case you might help the business perform user acceptance testing (UAT) (see below).

User acceptance testing (UAT)

User acceptance testing involves having the intended users of the system use the working software in a demo environment to validate it meets their needs and supports their business processes. Unlike a demo, in which the business analyst "uses" the software to show a pre-defined path, user acceptance testing unleashes users on the system. UAT is often structured around specific business process scenarios that form the business-facing test cases. UAT goes beyond functional testing in that it tests the software and business process in conjunction and helps flesh out any missing requirements or overlooked business process and training issues before deployment.

UAT can be led by quality assurance, business analysis, project management, or a primary stakeholder within the business. As a business analyst, you might be asked to provide input in terms of the business process scenarios. You might also be involved in vetting the new requirements that surface during UAT.

SOFTWARE DEVELOPMENT METHODOLOGIES

In addition to understanding the basics of business analysis, you should to have perspective on how the business analyst role fits within software development lifecycles and the tools you or your colleagues may be using. As you probably realize by now, a business analyst is never in a self-contained box. An awareness of the bigger picture is important to keep your responsibilities in context.

Software development cycles characterize how an organization approaches a project. As a business analyst, you'll likely work with (or interview for jobs that use) a variety of methodologies and software development cycles. You will want to be aware of the different methodologies, stay aware of current literature on new and existing methodologies, and, most importantly, understand the adaptations of the business analyst role within each methodology.

Waterfall

Hardly any organization is like to admit they are using "waterfall" anymore and this methodology is the butt of many jokes and passionate criticisms. The reality, however, is that many organizations are using some variation of the waterfall process. A waterfall methodology is exactly what it sounds like, each phase of the project (requirements, design, development, test, and implementation) occurring in linear order and concluding with a big splash at the end for delivery. While decidedly out of vogue, it can still be useful in very small projects.

More importantly, you should understand *why* it is out of vogue and the issues caused by a large, upfront requirements process un-vetted by design and implementation.

A core argument against a waterfall methodology is that stakeholders provide the best possible feedback on *working software* and by saving working software to the end of the process, a software implemented using a waterfall methodology often fails to meet stakeholder expectations. A second argument is based on the reality that today's organizations change and evolve rapidly. Since waterfall methodologies support a "lock down" of requirements early in a project, often 6-12 months before delivering working software, they inhibit the organization from effectively responding to change.

Many organizations' methodologies use more of the waterfall process than they would like to admit, so it's important to understand how to recognize a waterfall process when you see one.

Rational Unified Process (RUP)

The Rational Unified Process is an approach to software development that is "iterative, architecture centric, and use case driven" [7] . The essential principals of the RUP include attacking major risks early, maintaining a focus on quality throughout the project, and maintaining a focus on value. RUP focuses on creating an executable architecture early in the project lifecycle so subsequent project iterations can be built in interlocking sub-components.[8]

In the RUP, requirements are typically documented as use cases (see above discussion).This technique helps maintain a focus on value to the individual business stakeholders for each piece of functionality. The RUP is sometimes managed through IBM's Rational® tools. Oftentimes organizations employing a formal version of the RUP methodology have also invested in the Rational® Toolset and experience with Rational's RequisitePro™, Clear Case™, and/or ClearQuest™

---

[7] *The Rational Unified Process Made Easy.* Kroll and Krutchen. Page 3.
[8] *The Rational Unified Process Made Easy.* Kroll and Krutchen. Page 5.

might be necessary. Prior to Agile, RUP was the best-in-class iterative process. It still provides the foundational thinking behind many agile processes.

Agile

In 2009, Agile was making the transition from the latest fad in software development to an emerging, respectable trend and the business analysis community was beginning to get actively engaged in the discussion. This part of the book will likely date itself quickly, but if you are reading this in 2009 or 2010, it's worth developing a working understanding about agile and related processes as many organizations either think they are doing agile (and are wrong) or are thinking about starting to do agile.

At its core, agile methodologies favor short, incremental development to get working software in front of users as early as possible. Agile methodologies focus on collaboration, interaction, and responding to change over processes, documentation, and following a plan.[9]

To learn more about agile start with the Agile Manifesto[10], a short, fundamental text outlining the principles of agile software development, available for free online. Consider reading Scaling Software Agility: Best Practices for Large Enterprises by Dean Leffingwell for a thorough discussion of the variants

---

[9] *Agile Manifesto.* http://agilemanifesto.org/. 2001. Accessed 6/1/2009.
[10] http://agilemanifesto.org/

of agile, SCRUM, and XP methodologies and some advanced thinking on how to scale agile practices for large organizations and *Lean Software* by Mary Poppendeick for the fundamental principles governing agile practices.

The potential benefits of an agile methodology implemented in concordance with the core principles are significant, especially in terms of delivery efficiencies and team morale. However, there is little literature drilling into the cross-section of business analysis and agile software development. Much of the business analysis literature pays lip-service to agile but does not truly incorporate agile principles. Much of the literature on agile is development-centric and does not really acknowledge the complexity of the collection of activities involved in eliciting, analyzing, communicating, and validating requirements.

As of 2009, the roles of the "Agile Business Analyst" or "Agile Requirements" are just beginning to take shape. Ellen Gottesdiener has published a useful list of resources about Agile Analysis and Agile Requirements: http://www.ebgconsulting.com/agile-ModernAnalyst.pdf

Note: Variations of agile approaches exist, such as Scrum, Extreme Programming, and Feature-Driven Development. In addition, "Lean Principles" provide an even broader classification than agile, encompassing principles that apply within and outside software development with their roots in the manufacturing industry. There are significant philosophical and semantic debates over how to define these terms and processes. Most of the differences revolve around development techniques and not core principles and have very little direct impact on the business analysis role.

Mix and Match

Many organizations mix and match components of different methodologies to meet their organizational process needs. For example, as you are looking at job descriptions, you can't assume that just because they are looking for their business analysts to write use cases that they have implemented the RUP. They may be documenting the use cases upfront (i.e., waterfall) or in small pieces to be delivered incrementally (i.e., agile). Some organizations consciously choose to use bits and pieces of different methodologies and some believe they have implemented a specific process but in reality have not fully implemented it.

With all of that said, treat this section as a guide and to help you understand the possibilities, not to pigeon-hole an organization. You'll understand the most about an organization's software development methodology by talking to the people who use it day-to-day or reading their process documentation.

Tools

As a business analyst, you should be aware of the types of tools that many organizations use to optimize the requirements or software development processes.

You will use many tools as a business analyst and most of them are relatively easy to learn.

Word Processing, Spreadsheets, and Slide Decks

You can hardly find an office job anymore where Microsoft Office® skills are not either explicitly required or implied, and a business analysis position is no different. Knowing the basics of Word, Excel, and PowerPoint is necessary. Knowing how to exploit advanced features can give you a leg-up on your competition.

Requirements management tools

Requirements management tools are web-based or client-installed database applications that are used to support requirements management for a project or system. Organizations not employing requirements management tools often store requirements in documents or spreadsheets on a shared drive or Intranet document repository. Requirements management tools provide a cohesive structure for tracking and tracing requirements and often are used in organizations with formal and mature software development processes.

The features provided by tools vary widely, some providing the most support in the upfront product development cycle and vetting enhancement requests and some more integrated with the software delivery cycle. Some senior level positions will require or prefer expertise in a particular set of tools. Barring direct experience with a tool as a consumer or approver of requirements in a previous role, look for ways to familiarize yourself with the tools you see most often in job descriptions.

The basic features of a requirements management tool can include the following:

- Capturing requirements;
- Assigning attributes to requirements (such as priority, risk, cost, etc);
- Linking requirements (in hierarchies and across hierarchies);
- Analyzing the traceability of requirements;
- Configuration management of the requirements;
- Generating specifications (i.e., documents for review);
- Interoperability with other tools (such as design, modeling, and test case management tools).

For a comprehensive overview of the tools available and more detail on potential functionality offered, check out the INCOSE Requirements Management Tools Survey[11].

Many of the tools offer free trials. Downloading and exploring a tool a potential employer uses can be an excellent way to gain some experience and familiarity with the generalities of a tool. Be aware that most of these tools are highly customizable, so each employer

---

[11] http://www.incose.org/ProductsPubs/products/rmsurvey.aspx . Accessed 5/13/2009.

might use them a bit differently to support their requirements management process.

On the side of less formality (but not necessarily less structure), there is a growing number of web-based tools for managing software projects. Most tools include some aspect of requirements or document management. Teams are also beginning to use wikis to store requirements and forums to capture discussions about requirements.

As a new business analyst seeking a junior-level position, it is doubtful that familiarity with a tool will make or break a manager's hiring decision. Requirements management is usually owned by a senior-level professional in the group.

Defect tracking tools

Defect tracking (or bug tracking or issue management) tools are database applications used to manage issues with a system or project during the delivery cycle. It would be rare that a pure business analysis position would require specific tool expertise, but you should understand the available features and be able to speak to how you might use the tool as a business analyst.

A business analyst might use these tools for the following activities:

- Follow-up on defects in the requirements;
- Manage issues for a project or system;

- Manage enhancement requests (in organizations without a requirements management);
- Log issues or defects discovered in user acceptance testing;
- Prioritize defects.

Project management tools

Project management tools vary widely from scheduling and resource management tools such as Microsoft® Project to database-driven tools like Microsoft® Team Foundation Server and Rally Software®. There are also a variety of web-based project management tools that have basic requirements, issue, and project tracking capabilities and promote collaboration among team members. These are growing in popularity and you are more likely to find them in smaller companies or organizations with less formal processes.

With such a wide range of tools available, it is rare to find a business analysis position requiring specific expertise unless it involves actual project management responsibilities.

Modeling tools

Many business analyst positions require some modeling, whether in UML or just basic process diagrams and flow charts. Microsoft® Visio is by far the most common tool you will find in job descriptions.

Wire-framing tools

While Visio® can be used to build wireframes or mock-ups of screens to be implemented as part of the application, there are several other types of tools that are much more efficient. There is no one "standard" wire-framing tool to learn and therefore be qualified for a wide-range of positions. Even Microsoft® Word and PowerPoint provide some basic functionality for depicting the layout of a new screen.

The following is a short-list of tools with free trials, making them useful resources to experiment with wire-framing concepts and page layout:

- Axure: www.axure.com
- Mockup Screens: http://MockupScreens.com
- iRise: http://www.irise.com/
- Balsamiq: http://www.balsamiq.com/

Some UI-centric positions will look for Adobe® Photoshop or programming knowledge for creating functional user interface designs. While it can make sense to pair these two roles together, user interface and graphic design is outside the scope of this book.

Putting it to Practice # 4

Identify your positions of strength.
Congratulations on making it through this chapter! I threw a ton of information at you and you should be feeling somewhat overwhelmed.

At the beginning of the chapter I asked you to keep track of two categories as you went through. Now, I'd like you to make yourself a few lists so you can refer back to them later.

1. In your notebook, write down the concepts you understood the best and feel confident about.
2. Compare these to the list of areas that energized you in the previous chapter.
3. Are there overlapping items that fall onto both lists? Aspects of business analysis that you are excited about doing and have the knowledge to do?

Good. These are your *positions of strength*. It is easy to be over-whelmed or become down-trodden by what you don't know. This list represents the core skills or talents that you bring to this profession *as you are today*, no "ifs", "ands", or "buts". **Pat yourself on the back!**

What if I don't understand any of the concepts? If you did not understand any of the concepts in this chapter, it just means that you will need to educate yourself about the basics of business analysis. To build a list of strengths, focus primarily on what excited you about the role. You will want to leverage your passions to help your take your initial steps in experiencing the profession.

In this scenario, you might want to explore a short training program to accumulate BA knowledge. I recommend EBG Consulting's *Roadmap to Success* because it is virtual and self-paced, allowing you to work through the program slowly and apply what you've learned. You can find out more about *Roadmap to Success* at http://www.bridging-the-gap.com/roadmap-to-success.

Putting it to Practice # 5

Create a plan to build on your strengths
Let's take this a step further. For each strength, think of two or three things you can do to practice this strength to improve upon it. The goal is to take your strengths and build them into areas of expertise while building valuable business analysis experiences. Are these things you can start doing tomorrow? How about next week? Try to take an action to get started doing these things in the next few days.

Don't worry if you have trouble coming up with ideas. The next chapter is about exploring opportunities.

Putting it to Practice # 6

What do you need to learn?
In your notebook, write down the concepts you did not understand or where you do not feel truly confident about your understanding.

Take a moment now and put some context around these 'unknowns'. What is it you want to know? Do you need something defined? Do you want to understand how it works in the real world? What's the best way to find out more? For each of these, you will want to explore it further by reading, asking people questions, or searching online. In a few chapters, we will begin to put some more structure around questions you want to ask an experienced business analyst, so keep this list handy.

If you feel like the entire chapter feels like it belongs in this section, you will probably feel a bit overwhelmed right now. It can be a daunting task, but it will not be nearly as bad if you break it into pieces. Pull out the list of things that energized you about the role. Go back through the list of knowledge areas and look for ones that build on this excitement. It makes sense to turn this excitement into a learning opportunity by exploring the suggested resources for more information. Pick one area. Learn something about it and then go back to Putting it to Practice #5 and find a way to practice what you learned. Repeat.

Also, if you prefer learning via books as opposed to online, here are some book recommendations for mastering the BA fundamentals. Explore the options and select one that seems to best fit with where you are at and addresses what you need to learn. Most of these books can be read piecemeal and your favorites will become reference books you refer back to throughout your business analysis career.

Software Requirements Memory Jogger. By Ellen Gottesdiener. 2005.

Software Requirements, 2nd Edition by Karl Wiegers. 2003.

Chapter 3

Accumulating valuable business analysis experiences

Across all the interviews I did with successful business analysts, one theme emerged strongly above all others. Everyone who successfully made the transition did so because they were able to accumulate experiences either doing business analysis work or doing activities very closely aligned to business analysis work.

This section is about helping you gain those experiences to catapult yourself into a BA career. Don't worry if one section does not apply to your current situation, there should be another section that does.

You might also discover that you have had more BA experiences than you would have otherwise thought. As you recall these experiences, note them down. You'll want to use them later when re-working your resume.

TASKS TO TAKE ON IN YOUR CURRENT POSITION

If you pay close attention, you are likely to find opportunities in your current position or company to take on tasks that fall within the sphere of business analysis. These may not land in your lap. Instead, you'll need to be proactive in seeking out additional or different work assignments. Talk to your manager. Talk to trusted colleagues. Find out who needs help and offer up your new-found passion and knowledge.

What follows are some ideas of the type of activities to be on the look-out for. This list is by no means complete nor is it definitive. Instead use it as a guide or to trigger ideas that fit within your current organization or profession.

For the "techies"

If you are currently in a technical position (programmer, developer, IT support, quality assurance, etc), look for assignments that move you closer to the end-user of your software or provide the opportunity for you to take a broader perspective on a problem or solution.

> *"It was more of a progression than a choice."*
>
> *-David Wright, Business Analyst and author of* Cascade: Better Practices for Effective Delivery of Information Systems in a Multi-Project Environment

Look for customer-facing or internal-user facing exposure

The idea is to get is to get in contact with people who actually use the system you are currently building or, as a second-best option, the people who are responsible for marketing and selling to them. Get creative here. Maybe the business analyst is facilitating a meeting you can sit in on it. Maybe a product manager is facilitating a focus group you can observe. **Important consideration**: If you are still making this transition and you have implemented or know a lot about the code in this system, you might be tempted to respond to observations and questions in tech talk. If you are able to attend a meeting like this it is better to say nothing at all than to start talking code. You should be trying to learn to see the system and process from the viewpoint of the people who use it.

> *"As a direct consumer of requirements, you get an idea of what works and what doesn't."*
>
> *-Jonathan Babcock, Business Analyst and former QA professional*

Demo your software
Look for an opportunity to demo a piece of software you have built for anyone in the organization. Put your defenses aside and ask for honest feedback and new ideas. Throughout the demo ask questions to get their perspective on the software and better understand how it will be used. Not available in your organization? Conduct a demo for a friend or professional contact. You'll gather experience explaining your business and the product.

Become a critical consumer of requirements
Leverage your position as a consumer of requirements to learn more about the requirements process. You probably have already noticed that some requirements artifacts are much more helpful than others. If you are a developer, you likely find some requirements provide a crystal clear path and along with freedom to make important implementation decisions. Others constrain your efforts in challenging ways. As a QA professional, some requirements make it clear what and how to test, while others make it a challenge to identify what functionality would pass a test case.

Build on these opportunities to gain a deeper understanding of the requirements process. Investigate why a certain type of requirements is most useful to you. Consider helping the business analyst understand your perspective and possibly make some accommodations. BAs are people that respect good questions and thoughtful analysis. If you can find something they didn't think of (and you bring it up in a respectful way) they will be grateful and they will think highly of you.

Help select new software
Is your team or your business looking to select a new software package? Common needs include project tracking, time tracking, bug/issue tracking, source control repositories, intranet portals...the list goes on and on. Get involved in these projects in any way you can. Offer to analyze multiple tools against your teams

needs. Be sure to take some time and interview your teammates for requirements, analyze the process that the tool will support, develop a features or requirements list, and conduct a gap analysis. **Common mistake**: Do not treat this as an opportunity to get your own way but instead focus on facilitating discussion and agreement among multiple team members.

Do actual business analysis work
Let's face it, many companies do not have business analysts or, even if they do, they can be a scarce resource. Make a case for adding a business analyst to the staff (i.e., yourself) or help your company explore how this function would work by taking on a few typical BA tasks, such as a requirements document or the product backlog, for your next project.   Also consider that your organization might be fluid enough to allow you to do this in the context of your current work. Instead of jumping right to code, draft some requirements, create a test checklist, or simply summarize discussions in meeting notes. Be careful not to step on anyone's toes, but fill voids that you find as you learn about business analyst activities.

Solve a new problem or create a new opportunity
Use your detailed knowledge of the tool or application to solve a new problem for your customer or help them explore a new opportunity. Take some of your own time to brainstorm what could be possible with the technology you have, decide how that might fit within the customer's perspective, and talk to people

about your idea. Practice talking about the opportunity in non-technical jargon.

For those of you on the business side

If you are on the business side, whether as a subject matter expert or internal customer, try to get closer to the technologies and systems that you use day-to-day, obtain a broader perspective of these systems and the people who use them, or apply "analysis" techniques within the business processes of your department.

Become a subject matter expert (SME) on a project
Get involved in a technology project that directly impacts your functional area. Help the technology team craft a successful solution by envisioning the new application, providing input on your current processes, and providing your ideas about what the new system should do. Look for opportunities to document process flows and business requirements. If you are working with someone filling a business analyst role, ask to be part of the requirements process. Consider asking to help draft documentation, organize information, or other activities that help you step from the SME role into an analysis role.

Be careful not to step on any toes. It can help to be upfront about your career goals and ask for their help in building some experience.

How did I start my career as a business analyst?

One day, I was walking back to my desk when a senior BA in my company mentioned that a new position was opening soon. She recommended I apply for it.

Upon reflection, this was not a chance meeting in a hallway. I had done some things up to this time that had qualified me to become a business analyst.

I participated in requirements and use case review meetings. I found errors. I questioned details. I helped make the requirements better by being a critical consumer.

I established a new testing program to streamline the quality of an aspect of the system that was previously subject to ad hoc and unorganized testing from the business. I developed automated tests and organized business testing to create a structured UAT process. I essentially inserted myself between the business team and the development team to resolve issues that surfaced in UAT. I was learning to plan, communicate, and analyze.

I built strong product and stakeholder knowledge within my company. In QA I had been involved in more than 15 projects. I had worked with most of the project managers, product owners, business analysts and developers. I also knew most of our products inside and out.

On an important note, I did not learn the BA fundamentals until I landed my first BA position. I had the opportunity to learn the fundamentals on-the-job because of the experience and credibility I gained in QA. It's unlikely I would have found a BA position in another company at that time. But a year and a half later I had become a well-qualified BA and landed a position in another company.

You'll notice I used some of the techniques laid out in this book but not all. You should also select what works for you and your situation.

Be a facilitator SME
As a subject matter expert, you often have a lot of leeway in how you make decisions. Do you typically make all the decisions yourself based on your own expertise? Consider taking some steps to involve other people, facilitating discussions or even shadowing others if it's appropriate. You might find your decisions improving while you work on your elicitation, facilitation, and communication skills.

Become a guest SME for another group
Like a business analyst, an SME brings a special skill set to the project team and good SMEs are hard to find. Not all groups have perfect candidates or some groups are too over-worked to dedicate someone to a project. Find these opportunities and become their voice for a project. Offer to take decisions back to that group for consideration and bring their input back to the implementation team. You'll get practice eliciting, analyzing, communicating, and validating requirements.

> ***You can accumulate these experiences in any organizational situation. If your current employment situation does not support branching out, look for volunteer opportunities at your church, school, or professional association or even elements of your personal life.***

Own a technical project within your own group
Take a leadership role in a project such as an intranet, website, or software selection (see above). These projects will often require you to learn some technical jargon and possibly even communicate with an outside vendor about your needs. Depending on the project, you might also have the opportunity to define and communicate business requirements.

Facilitate a process-improvement session
Software projects automate business processes and business analysis involves business process as much as software requirements. By modeling an existing business process and facilitating discussions to determine a new and improved process, you will gain many BA experiences.

Help conduct an ROI analysis
Is your company or department considering a significant budgetary spend? Help your manager or another leader assess the impact of the investment. This type of analysis teaches you the importance of prioritization and will broaden your perspective regarding how your organization spends and makes money.

Become the point of contact for technical issues
In most organizations, there are people within the business who are the touch points with the technology team when issues arise, whether these are internal or externally facing. Get involved in this process. Learn to clarify and validate issues before submitting them to IT. Help the IT team through the resolution

process. You'll learn a lot about how the systems work, be exposed to more technology, and begin to bridge the gap between the business and technical teams.

Whether you are coming from business or IT

Work with business analysts
Most of the people I interviewed had opportunities to work with business analysts prior to becoming one. Leverage any opportunity you have to observe business analysts or partner with them on a team. As you build relationships, let them know about your career goals. This could create an opportunity to shadow them or help them with a business analysis task.

And don't overlook those consultants! If your company hires outside consultants for a software or process improvement project, it may be that any variety of business analysis tasks will be accomplished. Put yourself in a position to contribute or at least observe what they are doing. You can nearly always learn something from consultants as they have experiences from across multiple organizations to share. Typically there is no harm in building these relationships. Doing so could create a variety of learning opportunities. Go to lunch, linger after meetings, or catch them at the water cooler. Ask about their process. Get their perspective on the project and organization.

Tasks to take on in your personal life

Think you really want to be a business analyst? Consider some of these ideas for bringing BA-type responsibilities into your everyday life.

- Before making your next major purchase (car, house, or even a blender) do a complete requirements analysis. List out the features your want. Prioritize them. Compare your options against the features, balancing cost against benefits.

Kick it up a notch: Help an indecisive friend make their next purchase using BA fundamentals or interview your significant other and obtain sign-off on requirements before your next shopping trip.

- Rework an existing or broken process that is integral to running your household. Identify the beginning and the end. Identify your desired outcomes from the process (i.e., getting the kids to school with lunches). Analyze the detailed tasks using flow charts. Look for optimization or even automation opportunities. Complete a new proposed process and see the change through with your family or friends.

- Choose to purchase one piece of new software to use at home (taxes, tv, manage your library, etc). Define your requirements and inventory options.

Kick it up a notch: Try to build it for free with open source tools.

Define a new process.
Offer to help define and document a new process within your team or department.

Run a meeting
Facilitating meetings is one of the most basic skills a business analyst must have. The more experience you have running meetings, facilitating discussions, and publishing meeting notes, the more BA-like experiences you will accumulate. Look for these opportunities within your department, on cross-functional teams, or for special committees.

Take notes at a meeting
Even if there are not many opportunities to run a meeting, there could be opportunities to take notes. It can be a challenge to facilitate a meeting and get all the notes down on paper. Find a meeting where notes would be helpful (not just paperwork, but provide some value to the team). Offer to become the scribe. It's doubtful that anyone will challenge you for this responsibility. You'll be amazed at how quickly your listening skills improve when you take this on.

REFRAMING YOUR CURRENT TASKS

Some jobs may not provide the flexibility required for you to volunteer for new tasks, but that does not necessarily mean that there are no opportunities for you to gain business analysis experiences. Look for opportunities to reframe your current work as business analysis work.

Remember the core aspects of business analysis we discussed earlier:

- Elicitation
- Analysis & Specification
- Validation
- Communication

Each of these areas provides many fruitful opportunities for reframing an activity in terms of the business analysis role. You do not necessarily have to

> *"My first corporate job was at a call centre in the mid-nineties. After the initial few months of learning the ropes I started to become annoying by asking questions and challenging the process by proposing ways of doing things that I thought were better. And I tried to do this as a team player, rather than as the disgruntled rebel.*
>
> *Eventually this led me to being handed a number of projects to work on, and then to lead. The [BA] career evolved from there."*
>
> *-Craig Brown, PM and BA, author of http://www.betterprojects.net/*

take a project from beginning to end as a business analyst to gain a business analysis experience. Be creative and look for ways to piece together experiences.

Practice listening

The most critical skill you can refine and develop with respect to elicitation is listening. Listening means comprehending what you are hearing and letting the stakeholder know you have understood them. You can practice this skill using a technique called paraphrasing. After listening to someone speak on a topic say "Let me be sure I understand you, if I can put what you just said in my own words...." You'll get immediate feedback on how well you understood and you can use this technique repeatedly to improve your listening skills.[12]

Practice translating

As you improve your listening skills, you will begin to notice disconnects in conversations. Practice reframing what each person is saying to help them all understand each other better.

Practice asking questions

Whether or not you are responsible for facilitating a discussion, a well-placed question can serve to reframe the discussion and help others communicate. Ask questions when you believe something isn't clear or if people appear to be talking past one another.

---

[12] The suggestion to improve your active listening skills was offered by Doug Goldberg.

Organize a meeting

How well are your meetings organized today? Could you focus on improving them, making them more focused and efficient? Great business analysts facilitate productive meetings. What could you do to improve your meeting skills?

Observe someone

Could you create an opportunity to observe someone in their day-to-day work? If so, this is a great opportunity to practice elicitation skills, even if you are simply eliciting the requirements for how they use the system or perform a process today. Ask questions. Connect the dots. Take copious notes. And use your new understanding to create value for your organization.

Develop a systems and processes mindset

Business analysts tend to think clearly about who does what and how it is accomplished within an organization. Do you know how information flows through your organization and who is responsible for what? Do you have a good understanding of the business processes at work within your organization or various departments? Developing a thorough understanding of how businesses work is a powerful asset in obtaining opportunities to do business analyst work. This is a great exercise that can be applied to nearly any organization. Do this a few times in different organizations and you'll start to see commonalities that enable you to make useful generalizations and will help you work successfully in new organization, a key element of BA expertise.

Scope a project or activity

The concept of scope applies in many circumstances outside building software. Job descriptions represent scope. Any new project you take on has an explicit or implicit scope. Use these opportunities to practice "framing" a project. Write a one-page document or a summary email. Send it to your manager or other participants to confirm a mutual understanding.

Solve a problem and develop use case thinking

What opportunities do you have to solve problems? How do you approach these problems today? Would a bit of use case analysis help you? Everyday situations can often benefit from a bit of use case analysis. Describe the problem or scenario in a step-by-step flow of a use case, with alternate and exception flows to handle variations. Does this help you find a solution?

Improve something

Do you have the opportunity to improve something, even on the smallest of scales? A process, a template, or a piece of communication? Begin to take on a mindset of continuous improvement within your organization and you will begin to find more opportunities to take on slices of business analysis tasks.

Host a review or demo

Do you or your team create some sort of output that might be worth demoing? Has someone asked you a question about how something works? Use these opportunities to demo a process or review an output. You might be already participating in meetings that have core components of validation. Improve your demos by clarifying the viewer's perspective before the meeting and customizing your demo to meet their needs. This will help you become more externally focused and open to feedback.

Find opportunities to collaborate

Do you have opportunities to help people collaborate or be involved in any sort of collaboration project? Collaboration means communication, facilitation, and opportunities to listen and translate.

Putting it to Practice # 7

Create a plan for gaining business analyst experiences

Based on what you just read, brainstorm ideas for how you can take on business analysis tasks in your current employment (or non-employment) situation. Once you run out of ideas, look back through your positions of strength for additional ideas. Try to come up with at least 10 or 20 ideas.

Go through the list and pick one that feels the most comfortable but represents something you have not done before. Develop an action plan for achieving it in the next two weeks.

Now, select one that feels like a stretch and you feel will help you learn the most. Clarify this one. Visualize yourself doing it. Think about how it would feel to do it successfully. Imagine how proud you will be of yourself when you make it happen. Make a note and come back in a week or two and develop an action plan.

Putting it to Practice # 8

Log your BA experiences

For each business analyst experience, create an entry in your notebook explaining what you did and the impact it had on your organization. Describe how the task is a business analyst experience. How did the task go? Was the outcome positive or negative? What did you learn? What did you do well? What could you have done better?

And now that you have done this, what else seems possible?

I cannot stress how important it is to reflect on your experiences. The pure act of writing will help you clarify your thoughts and gain insights you will not have otherwise. Writing about what you are doing to become a BA will make you a better BA and accelerate your transition. As you write, you will likely surface other opportunities or recognize BA-related activities you are already incorporating into your day-to-day work.

Putting it to Practice # 9

Let one experience lead to another, and another....
Come back to this task after you have gotten your feet wet with some business analysis experiences and built some confidence.   Putting it to Practice #7 was specifically designed to help you select some tasks inside your comfort zone so you can build some confidence about your BA abilities. Staying in your comfort zone will not necessarily propel you into the BA profession.

Now you want to develop a plan to gain a wide-variety of business analysis experiences that will eventually qualify you for a BA position.

First, start a list of the experience you've had. Now, categorize them by the BA knowledge areas:

- Elicitation
- Analysis and Specification
- Validation
- Communication

Does this help you identify any gaps? If so, focus your next tasks to help fill these gaps.

Another way to identify gaps would be to look back at the knowledge areas in which you did not feel confident in your understanding. By now you should have done some reading of online articles or books to help you learn the fundamentals. Now that you know more about it, can you find some ways to practice it?

Continue to evolve this plan as you rack up experiences and build momentum.

Note: It's at this point in your career transition that a coach or a mentor might be exceedingly helpful. Either can help you apply the fundamentals to the business analyst experiences you are accumulating. A mentor or coach can also help you develop a personalized plan and stay motivated to keep on track even when you face difficulties or obstacles. The next chapter is on networking. As you begin meet more business analyst professionals, you might consider asking one to be a mentor.

Bridging the Gap also provides access to a network of qualified mentors to help new and potential business analysts take the next step in their careers. To find out more about the program visit http://www.bridging-the-gap.com and look for our Mentoring page.

Chapter 4

Professional networking

Professional networking is an inexpensive, productive way to learn about the profession and meet people that might help open opportunities for you. Networking can mean many things to many people. In the context of this book, professional networking is broadly defined as the set of activities to build mutually beneficial relationships with people in your profession or industry. By and large I would say that the majority of us under-network and this leaves us exposed to being uninformed and unemployed. Whether you are considering a career change or not, professional networking keeps you on top of your game. If you are seeking a career change, networking is essential.

Your goals for networking should include:

- Learning about the business analyst profession;
- Understanding the state of the profession in your location or target location;
- Establishing mutually-beneficial relationships with other professionals;
- Contributing to the professional community;
- Finding your next position.

Finding the next position is, by necessity, last on the list. Many people focus their networking here and lose out on the real opportunities. Instead, I suggest focusing your efforts on the first four and allow finding a position to be a by-product of these other activities.

There is nothing wrong with letting people know you are looking for a new opportunity (and if you are unemployed it's probably going to be difficult to hide that fact) but don't make it the object of your conversations. If people meet you, are impressed with you as a person and professional, and they know about a perfect opportunity for you, they are probably not going to hide it. Asking just makes them feel uncomfortable if they have to say "no."

Putting it to Practice # 10

Set some networking goals
Before jumping in to the how and what of professional networking, take a few minutes to write down what you would like to accomplish through networking. You can use the goals I defined above, but it will be more meaningful if you reclassify those goals to suit your personal situation. Make them more specific to you.

It may be worthwhile to reflect on what you have done so far. What you have learned about yourself through the experiences you have had? Consider networking a means to build on the strengths you have identified or fill in some of the knowledge or experience gaps.

Networking can easily become a time-sink or an end in itself. Taking a few minutes to clarify and focus can help you make sure you get the most out of this time-intensive activity.

PAY IT FORWARD

In any sort of networking activities, always keep the concept of "pay it forward" close to heart. While much of what we will be talking about in this chapter speaks to what you personally have to gain by participating in specific networking activities, keep your eyes and ears open for opportunities to contribute. Seek out questions or queries where you can help someone else, even if there is no direct benefit to you. Give without the expectation of receiving in return. With this mindset, opportunities will find of way of showing up in your sphere.

As you are conversing with people, do not simply focus on what you want to learn, but see if you can find a pain point or a need with which you can help the other person out. Always look for ways to make a contribution back to an organization or a relationship.

Key to paying it forward is being aware of what you can do to help.

- Simply ask if there's anything you can do to help.
- Listen carefully for needs and wants.
- Make generous, relevant offers to show your intentions.

What kinds of help can you offer? If you commit yourself to paying it forward, you will be amazed at the contributions you are able to make and the doors even the smallest of contributions will open for you. You have lots to offer. Consider the following:

- Make an introduction between two people that would benefit from meeting each other.
- Review an article, paper, or resume.
- Mock-interview a fellow colleague looking for a new position.
- Send relevant information to someone (website, article, book recommendation, etc).
- People engaged in online networking appreciate you making an effort to continue the conversation. Find ways to participate in those conversations or share information with your network of online influence. (This will be discussed in detail in the Online Networking section below.)
- Provide support. Sometimes people just need to hear how you've helped them. Taking the time to write a personal thank you (via email or a traditional thank you card) for something you learned or how you value the services they provide can be a reward in and of itself.

Be confident that you have something to give and that it has value. You do. You have power beyond measure to help other people. Your own beliefs to the contrary are your only constraint.

Putting it to Practice # 11

Be ready with what you can do to help
Even if you are nodding your head to the above, nothing commits you to making an offer than having prepared a list of ideas. Take a few minutes and think about how you can help others.

NETWORKING EVENTS

What events should I attend?

Your best networking opportunities will come from local professional associations. In particular, if you have a local IIBA® chapter, you'll want to start attending their meetings. If you don't have an IIBA® chapter, look for professional meetings in related professions (including business process engineering, product management, project management, quality assurance, or software development) as it's quite likely you'll find business analysts at these other meetings...maybe even others who want to collaborate to start an IIBA chapter!

A second group of networking opportunities will come from process-specific groups. In particular, Agile and SCRUM tend to have local groups and people from a broad range of software development disciplines attend their meetings.

Consider industry-specific groups where you will meet people from a variety of professions but working in the same industry. These groups could be especially helpful if you plan to leverage your industry expertise to help you transition into a business analyst role.

Finally, if you are currently unemployed or have a lot of flexibility in your schedule, also research local career or job networking groups in your area. These groups help people "in between opportunities" stay connected and up-to-date.

There are several valuable resources for finding local events, most of them online. Here are a few of my favorites.

- Meet-up: www.meetup.com. This site allows local groups and organizers to post events for a small fee. You will find a variety of groups, not all of them geared toward professional topics.
- Local LinkedIn groups.
- Web searches for your location and "networking events" or "groups" or "meetings".

Once you attend a few events, it will be easier to keep up-to-date and informed. Just ask attendees what other meetings they attend.

What do I do at a networking event?

Many people are intimidated by networking meetings. I have never been great at meeting new people, but since I started as an independent consultant I've learned a few techniques for turning these meetings into positive experiences.

- Lower your expectations. Oftentimes networking meetings are difficult because our expectation (or hope or goal) is to find a job. This is unrealistic and setting that goal will not only cause you continual disappointment, but it will cause you to initiate inappropriate conversations and actually make that outcome less likely.
- Set a reasonable expectation of say, meeting one person with whom you'd like to have a more

involved conversation and obtaining their contact information.

- Arrive early. Most networking tends to happen before the meeting starts. Some groups are tight and most people know each other. Other groups have just as many first-timers as regulars. Ask a few people some basic questions like:
  - o Is it your first meeting?
  - o Have you been before? What's it like?
  - o Share information you might know about the speaker or the topic. Get the other person's perspective.
  - o What do you do?
  - o How did you find that opportunity? (You will learn so much by making this question a habit whenever anyone mentions a new opportunity, new job, new contract... anything.)
  - o What methodologies do you use?
- Introduce yourself to at least 1-2 new people. Force yourself to do this if necessary.
- Plan to linger a bit. After evening meetings, people tend to rush out to get back home and to their families. I am always surprised at this because there is so much to talk about after the meeting. The people who linger want to meet people so don't be tentative about initiating a conversation about what the presenter had to say.
- When you meet someone interesting, explain your situation and ask if they would be willing to meet with you and share their experience.

- Take pride in who you met and what you learned. Even if the content was not all that great, you probably learned at least one new thing or it prompted you to think about something differently.
- The next morning, email anyone you met, noting an interesting aspect of your conversation and expressing your interest in meeting them to share their experiences. If you can attach something of value, say a link to a website or the title and author of a book you recommended, all the better. Emailing them soon ensures they have a second trigger to remember you before they forget you and increases your chances of a scheduling the follow-up discussion.[13]

Putting it to Practice # 12

Plan your networking calendar for the next 2 months
It's time to find networking events that you can attend in the coming months. If you are currently employed and relatively satisfied, a good goal might be to find an average of 2 events per month. If you are currently unemployed or want to find a new position in the next 3 months, consider setting a goal closer to 2 events per week.

Your goal within each meeting should be to find one person you would like to speak with further, getting

---

[13] This set of suggestions is heavily influenced by One Call Away: Secrets of a Master Networker, by Jeffrey W. Meshel with Douglas Garr. 2005.

their contact information, and requesting the meeting. (More on what to do in that meeting is below, in the informational interviews section.)

Regardless of how many events you attend per week, focus on quality over quantity. Quality connections. Quality conversations. Quality learning opportunities from the presentations.

LEVERAGING THE CONNECTIONS YOU ALREADY HAVE

Networking is great, but often you are starting from "zero" at a new event. Not all events are easy to break into. Think about how you might be able to leverage the people you already know (and who know you personally) for help. Again, it's important not to make this a generic "I'm looking for a job" request. Many people you know will not be able or willing to help you find a job, at least directly. But they would probably introduce you to someone they know so you can learn more about a profession.

Consider the following ideas to identify the potential connections.

- Do you know any business analysts? Have you worked with anyone who held business analyst responsibilities in the past?
- Ask colleagues and friends if they know of anyone who might be interested in sharing their experience. Stress in these communications that

you are not just looking for a job, you are looking to learn.

- Ask everyone you meet if they can recommend anyone else you should speak with. Oftentimes people are happy to introduce you to a colleague or their manager, especially if they know you will be using this as a learning opportunity and not just asking for a job.
- Broadcast a request on LinkedIn.

If you own or can borrow *The PathFinder*[14], there is an excellent inquiry called "The Networking Game". It essentially asks you to list everyone you know personally and professionally, rate them based on how committed they are to your success, and identify how they might be able to help you. This is a great exercise because it broadens your mind about the people in your network, helps you become intentional about your networking, and helps you adjust to the idea of asking for appropriate help.

Putting it to Practice # 13

Set-up 2 or 3 informational interviews
Contact 2 or 3 business analysts you already know and ask if they would be willing to share their experiences. Explain that you are considering pursuing a career in business analysis and would like to ask them a few questions about their experience in the profession.

---

[14] The Pathfinder: How to Choose or Change Your Career for a Lifetime of Satisfaction and Success. Nicholas Lore. Page 337-345.

> ### *People will say yes!*
>
> Megan Herlihy successfully made the transition from marketing communications to business analysis in the spring of 2009. She started in her "comfort zone" by asking former colleagues for informational interviews and eventually graduated to asking people she met at networking events. She encourages you to get over the intimidation and focus on interviewing people you really find value in meeting.
>
> Megan did 1-2 interviews per week for a few months and reports that 80-90% of the people she asked agreed to meet with her.

INFORMATIONAL INTERVIEWS

The informational interview provides the "action" you need to initiate or build on a relationship. For any business analyst you know or meet through your professional networking, asking if you can meet with them to learn more about the profession provides an option for a subsequent discussion.

People love to talk about themselves and you want to learn about being a business analyst. If you meet someone and hit it off, sincerely ask if you can email them or call them to talk a bit more about what they do. Stress that you are evaluating whether business analysis is the right career choice for you (or that you are simply trying to learn from successful BAs) and you'd appreciate the opportunity to ask them a few questions. Conduct as many as you possibly can— you'll learn something different from everyone, even if it's simply the advantage of a new perspective. And as you build experience interviewing business analysts, consider expanding your interviews to other professions to gain outside perspectives on business analysis.

When setting up an informational interview, be as flexible as possible with the other person. If it's reasonable, offer to meet them in their office, over their lunch hour, or outside their normal working hours for coffee or breakfast. I consider coffee meetings the best alternative as the cost of a coffee is nominal...you can either pick up both coffees or not, but it's not an economical inconvenience either way. (If you are really strapped for cash and even buying two coffees is out of the question, suggest their office or find local libraries with private meeting rooms you can reserve.)

The questions you ask should be personal, in the sense that you are personally interested in the answers, but also professional, in that you should not ask someone you just met on a professional level questions they may not be comfortable answering.

You will get the most out of this activity if you develop a list of questions that address your strengths and knowledge gaps. For example, if you have no experience with requirements management tools, you might consider asking your interviewees what tools they have used and what the merits were of each. This is your opportunity to expose yourself to "BA talk" and get some free informal training. Alternatively, if you feel you are a strong listener, you might want to ask how they use listening skills in their day-to-day work, providing you with more ideas for gaining business analysis experiences or rephrasing experiences you have already had in business analyst language.

Here are some possible questions you may consider:

- What are the main responsibilities of a business analyst? What is a typical day like?
- What are the pros/cons of being a business analyst? Is there growth in this field?
- Who does a business analyst typically report to?
- Who does a business analyst typically work with?
- How would you describe the ideal candidate for a business analyst position? What skills are required?
- Why did you yourself decide to become a business analyst?
- How did you find your first business analyst opportunity?
- Are the BA training programs useful, especially for those without experience? Do you recommend any?
- What BA resources (web sites, books, tools, etc.) would you recommend?

- What software development models are you familiar with (Waterfall, Agile, etc.)? Which do you prefer? Why?
- What local meetings do you attend? What are the benefits of them?
- What kinds of tools should a new business analyst learn about?
- How else do I find additional information? Who would you suggest I contact?[15]

Putting it to Practice # 14

Preparing for your informational interviews

By now you should have a few meetings set-up. To get the most out of these meetings, take some time to prepare. If you have completed the previous tasks, you will already have a list of questions about the profession you want answered. Go through this list and put yourself in the position of an experienced BA. How can you phrase the question to get the most insightful answers from someone who is doing what you would like to be doing?

Gaps. Go back through the list of knowledge and experience gaps you have uncovered? What could you learn from an experienced BA that would help you take another step forward?

Personalize it. Research what you can about the person you will be interviewing. At a minimum review

---

[15] This set of questions is largely from a list provided by Megan Herlihy.

their LinkedIn profile and any information readily available through a web search engine. Think up a few questions specifically suited to their background and experience.

ONLINE NETWORKING

Another valuable way to expose yourself to new ideas and people is to network online. There are a variety of websites and social networks catering to nearly every profession and niche interest. People who join these networks are often looking for like-minded individuals with whom to share ideas. By participating in a few online networks you will begin to build an online profile of yourself as a professional business analyst.

An additional benefit of participating in online networking communities is that you can control your online presence. Recruiters and hiring managers often

> *"I learned more in the last year and a half than I would have in ten without social media."*
>
> *-Jonathan Babcock, Business Analyst and blogger (http://www.practicalanalyst.com)*

search online about candidates before making hiring decisions. If you haven't already, take a few minutes and put your name into any web search engine. What are the results?

Are your search results selling you? A few comments on blogs and publicly available forums can put some relevant, insightful information about you in these search results. This shows that you are contributing to your own professional development by making use of the available resources.

Finally, if you are open to or specifically seeking to relocate, you might focus more attention on online networking activities to connect with people in your target location(s). Imagine moving to a new city and already knowing several professionals in the area. It happens!

Social Networks

Not all social networks are created equal and there is no one-stop shop. It's a good idea to explore multiple options and find the sites that best sync with your online inclinations.

Here's a short list of social networking sites that focus on business analysis and related topics.

- http://www.modernanalyst.com
- http://requirementsnetwork.com/
- http://www.requirements.net
- http://requirements.seilevel.com/
- http://community.theiiba.org

- http://stickyminds.com

These are some good starting places to get a feel for what the BA profession is doing online. Within them you'll find profiles of individuals, links to blogs and other sites, links to companies that serve the BA profession and much more.

Another great resource for online discussions and links to articles is LinkedIn (http://www.linkedin.com). The power of LinkedIn for interacting with other professionals is in the groups. As of this writing, the following groups were productive and active in the business analyst space:

- ModernAnalyst
- BA Forum
- Business Architecture
- Agile Business Analyst
- Starting a business analyst career

This will be an ever-changing list. New groups become active every day. I keep my groups public so feel free to check out my Linked profile (http://www.linkedin.com/in/laurabrandau) for what I'm currently active in or use LinkedIn's search feature to find groups related to your specific interests.

Blogs

Blogs augment social networking sites by providing forums for one or more individuals to publish their ideas. There are several excellent blogs about business analysis and you can learn about nearly any topic by reading blogs. Content on blogs tends to be more experience-driven and less formal and structured than you might find in an article or book. Reading blogs is a great way to connect with other business analysts, learn from real-life experiences, and participate in discussions about current topics.

> **Online Tip**
>
> When commenting on a blog or forum, make it easy for people to find out more about you and contact you by including a URL. If you do not have your own website or blog, link to your LinkedIn profile.

What follows is a short-list of blogs by business analysts about business analysis. The writing available in this space is expanding every day. To get a feel for BAs in the blogosphere, you can start here and follow links to other resources from their posts or blogrolls. If you'd like to research a specific topic, consider using Google's blog search to search for that topic.

• Trials and Tribulations of a Business Systems Analyst: http://it.toolbox.com/blogs/business-analyst/

- Practical Analyst by a working business analyst, Jonathan Babcock: http://practicalanalyst.com
- BA Mentor, a site focusing on the business analyst fundamentals: http://businessanalystmentor.com/
- Tips for Effective Communication between Business and IT by Pat Ferdinandi: http://sbditipsblog.wordpress.com/
- Requirements Defined hosted by Seilevel, a professional services organization focused on creating software requirements: http://requirements.seilevel.com/blog/ (Seilevel's message board can also be a valuable resource)
- Bridging the Gap between Business and IT by myself with frequent guest posts by fellow BAs: http://bridging-the-gap.com
- Resources for Business Analysts, a membership site with loads of free resources about BA knowledge, by Geri Winters: http://www.resourcesforbusinessanalysts.com/

How to participate

Most social networks have forums and this is a great place to start getting to know a site. Reading the archives will give you a sense of the conversations. You can lurk for awhile, but it's through active participation (comments on blog posts, responses to questions, etc.) that you'll get the most value out of online networking. You will learn so much more and think so much more clearly when you capture your thinking in textual form and expose it to the community for response and feedback.

Making one-on-one connections

General information and discussions are great and you can learn a lot online, but the real power of online networking comes when you make one-to-one connections with individuals.

When you encounter someone online that you share particular interests with or have interesting online dialog, send them a personal message. Most social networking sites have a way to send another member an email through the site. You might have to dig a bit to find it. If you can't get in touch with the person through the site you are on, check and see if they have a LinkedIn profile. Most people do and set their profiles to enable them to receive message from other members, even if you are not connected.

Take care in crafting your emails. Start with a sentence or two thanking them for some value they've provided or summarizing your interest based on discussions that have been made in these public forums. Then ask a question or two that you are legitimately interested in. Does this sound weird to you? I bet it does. But let me tell you...it works. Just like people are willing to share their knowledge in an informational interview, people are very often happy to help when you can be clear about the help you need. When you get a response (this won't always happen, but you'll be surprised how often it does happen) try to continue the dialog either via email or via the phone. These new contacts are great ways to conduct "informational interviews" with a broader set

Laura and Linda on LinkedIn

I met Linda online via LinkedIn. She requested a connection. I found her profile interesting. I was just starting to look for consulting work. I suggested a phone call. This initial contact blossomed into two phone conversations threaded together by a series of emails and Tweets. I have helped Linda – made an introduction and sent along a few pieces of useful info. She has helped me – exposure to new projects and a potential blog contributor. I have definitely grown because of the connection and, especially, making the connection *personal*.

of people than may be available in your locale or that may show up at the same networking events that you do.

Another way to find interesting people online is to search for professionals in your area with related job titles. Contact them directly, explaining your situation and asking if they'd be willing to meet you and share their experiences. You can also use LinkedIn to find non-local individuals and to schedule a phone conversation. This might be necessary if you are truly in a remote area. Otherwise, I'd suggest limiting this type of extended search to people with whom you share multiple commonalities, for example if they made the transition to business analysis from the same career you are currently in or you share a common industry background. Well-targeted and thoughtful contacts through LinkedIn have a much higher success rate than haphazard form letters.

Twitter

There is much ado about Twitter these days. Twitter is an element of social media that can be used to keep in touch with fellow professionals and stay up-to-date on online conversations.

If you are not familiar with Twitter, here are the basics:

- Sign-up for an account with a handle and some very basic profile information (http://www.twitter.com).
- Post "tweets" of 140 characters or less.
- Choose to follow other Twitter users. View their Tweets.
- Respond to tweets (i.e., @LLBrandenburg you are boring us with the twitter basics).
- "Retweet" other Tweets to promote messages started by others (i.e., RT @LLBrandenburg you are boring us with the twitter basics).

And that's about it. It's deceptively simple.

I'd recommend exploring Twitter if you haven't already just to get a feel for it. This may resonate with you as an outlet or it may not.

There are three main Twitter usage patterns:

1. Consume information / learn cool things / keep up-to-date.
2. Broadcast information / share cool things.
3. Converse with others.

Most Twitter users combine patterns. Some just broadcast and these people tend to get an "unfollow" rather quickly unless the information they are broadcasting information is compelling. For example, I follow a couple of news channels just to keep up-to-date, but I would not follow a blogger who only posts links to their own content.

As you explore Twitter as part of your professional development and online professional profile building, consider the following guidelines:

- If you want to carry on a lot of personal or what might be considered unprofessional chatter using Twitter, strongly consider two profiles.
- Give people a reason to follow you. Be interesting. Post interesting information, interesting experiences. Retweet good links.
- Ensure what you Tweet resonates with your professional personality and how you would want potential employers and co-workers to view you. They may be reading.
- Your Tweets often show up in search results too. Even if you have two profiles, be careful what you Tweet!

Twitter can be a productive part of establishing and maintaining connections. When I follow people in my local area I tend to have a better idea what they are up to in between face-to-face meetings, bringing a stronger connection to even infrequent in-person meetings.

Putting it to Practice # 15

Update your LinkedIn Profile and other relevant profiles
Take stock of the online profiles you already have. How would they be viewed by potential employers or other professionals? Do they clearly state your intentions about becoming a business analyst? Do they represent your professional persona? Take some time and clean-up your profiles, paying special attention to your LinkedIn profile.

Putting it to Practice # 16

Explore online resources and start an online information routine
Begin incorporating online business analyst resources into your daily or weekly routine. Check out the resources mentioned in this section that interest you the most. Leave a few comments or even start a discussion. Test the waters and engage in the community.

As you explore, select at least 2-3 resources to become part of your online information routine. If you consider online networking to be a core part of your professional development, you might choose to keep up with 10-20 blogs. Personally, I have over 20 business analysis and project management blogs fed into my home page and I know this is a small snapshot of the available content.

Set aside a time to check in on these sites regularly, set up alerts, or sign-up for their RSS feeds. It does not matter *how* you choose to stay informed, only that you develop a method that works for you.

Advanced Online Networking
Is the above not enough for you? There are a few more things you can do to take your online professional presence to the next level.

- **Start a blog**. If you have a lot to say and want an independent platform to share your experiences, consider starting your own blog. You should be prepared to post 1 or 2 articles per week. Setting up a blog is also a great way to stay informed of or gain exposure to the basics of web technology.

- **Guest post on other blogs**. Writing articles for other blogs is a great alternative if you don't want to post at least once or twice per week but would still like to publish your professional thinking. Many bloggers host guest posts as a way to keep their content fresh and their publication pipeline full. Some of the social media sites also host blogs as well, specifically http://www.modernanalyst.com and http://requirementsnetwork.com/.

- **Become a power networker on LinkedIn**. Every person you are "connected with" on LinkedIn opens up your LinkedIn profile to more people, increasing the chances you'll show up in other people's search results. Use the search functionality to find relevant connections and personalize your connection requests for a better response rate.[16]

KEEPING UP THE MOMENTUM

A common pitfall of networking is to meet a bunch of new people and then lose touch with them over time. Establishing the initial connection is the most difficult aspect of networking. Given this, you would do well to find a way to stay in touch with the people you meet and continue to build on those relationships.

As you continue in your professional development, you will most likely have opportunities to share something with someone you have met or learn something new from them.

How you do stay in contact is a matter of personal preference and you might choose different methods for different people. Some ideas:

- Send thank you cards to all your informational interviewees. This is a nice and unexpected touch that reminds them of your conversation.
- Send out a regular emails summarizing what you've learned or what you've been up to.

---

[16] I personally am not a fan of "connecting" on LinkedIn with people I haven't made some sort of connection with otherwise. But I don't represent the norm. Many people use LinkedIn connections to expand their network.

- Let your new contacts know when you have found your first BA opportunity! They deserve the opportunity to share in your success!
- Send along useful information. Continue to "pay it forward." Harness what you've learned about what your new contacts need and send along useful information. Even consider doing a little independent research and forwarding it along.
- Seek out people you have met with the next time you see them at a meeting. Say hello and check in on how things are going.

Staying in contact over the long-term will trigger their memory about you and your career change if an opportunity comes up. It is not necessary to ask for it, but it is necessary to keep yourself in front of them in a way that is not annoying.

A FINAL WORD ON NETWORKING

Networking (online and off) can be a consuming and sometimes distracting activity. It's important you set personal goals for what you want to achieve through networking and regularly assess yourself against these goals. Are you learning? Are you meeting with the right people? Are you finding new opportunities? Are you asking the right questions? Are you building real relationships with the people you are meeting?

Putting it to Practice # 17

Craft a personalized networking plan

The tasks included in this chapter were intended to give you a flavor of the types of professional networking activities that are valuable for potential business analysts. After a few weeks of exploring online resources, attending networking events, and conducting a few informational interviews, return to this chapter with a fresh perspective. Evaluate the results you have achieved against the goals you laid out in the beginning.

- What activities provided the most benefit?
- Where could you improve on how you engage with others?
- What have you learned?
- What fresh perspectives did you find?

Now craft your own go-forward plan. It might look something like this:

Event/ Activity	Frequency	Intended benefit	Most recent result
IIBA meetings	1/month	Meet BAs for interviews. Learn about the profession through presentations.	Met Don, who agreed to interview. Learned about use cases.
Info Interviews	1/week	New BA perspectives. New BA relationships.	Learned about BA experience in agile from Tracy. Fresh perspective on long documents.

Check out Modern Analyst	1/week	Stay up-to-date on BA literature. Explore BA concepts as part of self-education.	Found an article on use cases that I used to draft a new process.
Twitter	2/day	Build BA relationships. Stay fresh on new content.	Found post on domain models. Met John for info interview over the phone.
....			

This should not be a static list. As you grow professionally, the activities you find value in might also change. Review this periodically and adjust based on your goals and what is working for you.

Chapter 5

Is business analysis your passion?

If you've been actively participating in the activities up to this point, you've established a broad understanding of the business analyst's role and learned what it's like. You've tried it on in your current job or via activities in your personal life. You've met at least a few business analysts and heard what they had to say. Maybe some of it resonated with you.

Does it fit?

Are you ready and committed to start a business analyst career?

If so, congratulations! Deciding to make a career change is a difficult decision and making the commitment to forge onto something new for your own personal and professional well-being, is a significant step. Well done. Pat yourself on the back.

You'll be tempted to start looking and applying for jobs and most likely you already have. But before you get too far down this path, please stop for just a few minutes. Grab your notebook and do a bit of writing.

- Why does this change feel right?
- What are your expectations from this change? (for yourself, your family, your finances)
- What is your most important expectation?

- What are you going to have to give up to make this change? (friends at work, a secure job, work from home hours, etc)

Are you still committed?

It's OK to say no. But if you really felt committed before you thought through these questions, I'd challenge you to consider if you are letting your fears or your passions drive your commitment.

For everything we take on, we must give something up. This can be positive or negative, but it will be a change. Even letting go of negative things can require some grieving. Think about people who struggle with cigarettes and alcohol.

What are you addicted to in your current position that could hold you back? It's best to be aware of this now and face it head on rather than have it rear its ugly head in the middle of an interview for your dream job when someone inevitably asks you "what will you miss about your current job?"

Still in?

Awesome. Let's get to work finding you a business analyst position.

Chapter 6

What kind of business analysis job is right for you?

In this chapter we'll explore common types of business analyst positions and help you determine which one (or ones) will be the best fit with your talents, current skill set, and career goals.

WHAT TYPES OF BA POSITIONS ARE THERE?

The first thing to note is that BA jobs come in all kinds of flavors. While the IIBA is doing some great work to solidify the profession, we are a long way from having a steadfast definition that is shared across multiple contexts. Even once we do there will most likely continue to be specialization within industries, technologies, and process areas.

> *"Specific system knowledge or industry experience, combined with relevant BA-type experiences, can help a new business analyst land a job."*
>
> *-Ted Hellmuth, IT Recruiter, Division Director, Robert Half Technology*

Let's first look at some of the common types of BA jobs and then help you figure out in what direction you want to head. This list and the descriptions are not mutually exclusive. Positions will tend to fit into more than one category.

Industry-focused

Some business analysis jobs focus on specific industries and require years of experience and in depth familiarity with that industry. This is not all that different from other professions where industry experience can also be a requirement. There is a lot of debate as to whether or not this is particularly relevant to this profession as a talented business analyst can get up to speed on knowledge areas fairly quickly and elicit business requirements regardless of that knowledge. Regardless of what side of the debate you find yourself on, in reality many hiring managers show a strong preference for industry expertise. I've seen industry experience be a factor most often in the following industries: oil and gas, telecommunications, real estate, and insurance.

Tool or Process-specific

Other business analysis jobs require expertise in specific tools or software packages. Some examples include implementing complex applications such as enterprise resource management, customer relationship management and accounting systems. These positions value detailed understanding of a specific software or business process because this understanding helps BAs be efficient in understanding the problem domain, presenting possible solutions, and leveraging the full capabilities of the chosen solution.

Oftentimes you will be working with stakeholders to map the problems they want to solve and figuring out how to solve that problem with a tool they have already made an investment in. Some of these jobs require more technical know-how and involve configuring the tool for the client, importing data, and supporting administrative activities. These roles are found most often within consulting companies as few organizations find it necessary to hire on this expertise on a full-time basis. However, very large organizations might hire a tool expert in-house.

Background experience as a user, subject matter expert, or implementer of an application can help you qualify for an entry-level business analyst position that requires specific tool or process expertise. To find out if your expertise is relevant in your target locations, try using the product names in job search engines and seeing what types of roles you find. Tool-specific BA jobs are very likely to be titled something other than a "business analyst", with "project manager" or "implementation engineer" being common examples. These are often commonly found to be blended roles, which are discussed a bit later.

Product BAs

Some BA roles are involved in creating customer-facing software products, including web-based applications and downloadable software applications. The main stakeholders will often be from the product and marketing groups. In this role, the BA might also help bridge the gap between the product/marketing group and the internal processes needed to support the product in customer service or accounting. Sometimes there is a separate BA group or stakeholder with this responsibility.

While BAs in these types of jobs will often have external customer interaction, the amount of direct interaction with users of the system can be much more limited than when working with internal users. As a result, working on a product can feel more like a hypothetical journey. While there are often opportunities to get feedback, it is much more limited and comes in the form of focus groups, beta tests, usability tests, and demos. Sometimes the product or marketing manager "owns" this communication loop but most often the business analysts are involved, at least as an observer.

BA Consultants

There are several organizations who offer BA consulting services either as a stand-alone service or as part of a larger consulting packaged service. Companies may consult with clients on specific tools or processes (see above), specialize in custom software development, address business process changes, or help in any area of the business. As a BA within a consulting company, your time will be billed hourly to a client and you will likely be required to be onsite at the client's office. This could require travel (up to 100% in some positions). Alternatively there are smaller, local consulting companies in some of the major cities where you might be able to do primarily local consulting.

Consultants often have several years of experience and unless you bring a unique combination of past experience and knowledge that the consulting company needs to meet the needs of a specific client, it's unlikely that you'll find these positions as a new business analyst. Consultants are blessed with the diversity of work that is a byproduct of working with several organizations each year and the requisite pain and suffering that goes with such work.

Some business analysts choose to be independent consultants. As an independent consultant, you take on short-term jobs, often on a part-time basis, to serve specific business needs. This is a lot like working for a larger consulting company, except that you are responsible for the end-to-end operations of running a business, from sales and marketing to accounting.

Contract BAs

Contract work most often involves a full-time, short-term commitment to a specific organization. The company hiring a contractor may need specific expertise for a short period of time or, for some other reason, cannot or will not commit to a full-time hire. Many companies today are using contract-to-hire arrangements to "try out" a candidate before making a full-time hire.

Contract work will often be specific and focused. You might be assigned to one or two projects and are not likely to have broad responsibilities within the department. As a contractor on a team of full-time employees, you may not be involved in team meetings and other company events. You most likely will not have as much access to mentoring and training opportunities as the company only plans to have you on for a short time. However, you can gain valuable experience, access to a new company, and it can be a foot in the door to a full-time opportunity.

At first blush, it can seem that contractors make more money than full-time employees. Be sure to factor the additional taxes and lack of benefits out of the higher hourly rate to make a fair comparison.

BA Blends

Many organizations, intentionally or not, blend the business analysis role with another role in the organization. This could become more common as different methodologies are switching up the make-up of traditional IT teams. Here are some of the more common blends.

Project Manager / Business Analyst

On the best of teams, project management and business analysis responsibilities go hand in hand and the line between the two is often gray. Combining the two roles into one person means that in addition to your business analysis responsibilities you will be accountable for scope, schedule, cost, and managing the implementation through deployment. This is a common blend even in larger organizations that simply choose not to separate the two roles. If you are looking to transition from a project manager into a business analyst role, these blends can obviously provide good BA experiences and you'll likely be well-qualified for the positions.

Business Analyst / Quality Assurance
This is another common blend founded on the premise that those who defined the requirements are in the best position to test against the requirements. There is some validity to this, especially in smaller organizations. Both functions share common values—a drive for high-quality software. And when one is vacant, people in the complementary role tend to fill the gap. I've seen great testers become business analysts because no one was defining requirements (and therefore they did not have any specifications to test against) and great business analysts test simply because they were driven to see their requirements through to "done."

Product Manager
Often hidden within the job description of a product manager are responsibilities like "define business requirements" or "liaison with the technical team on product specifications." This often happens in organizations with no defined business analysis role. If you have the industry experience for the product manager role (which is often most important) this can be a great transition role for you. But be forewarned that product managers have significant responsibilities and you will often be left with inadequate time to really specify and analyze the

detailed requirements the way you would want to as a business analyst.

Information Architect (UI Design / Content / Business Analyst)
Many consulting firms helping companies design content-rich websites and software and employ Information Architects (IA) as part of the design process. The Information Architecture Institute defines IA as:

- "The structural design of shared information environments.
- The art and science of organizing and labeling web sites, intranets, online communities and software to support usability and findability.
- An emerging community of practice focused on bringing principles of design and architecture to the digital landscape."[17]

IA positions can vary in their focus, some emphasizing how the content is organized and some emphasizing the user experience and usability. Within the scope of the IA responsibilities is often being the liaison with the development team, whether through formal requirements or some other form of communication and specification.

---

[17]   http://iainstitute.org/en/learn/resources/what_is_ia.php. Accessed 6/5/2009.

Developer / Programmer Analyst
Some organizations require their developers to gather requirements from the "customer", often a product manager or internal subject matter expert. Roles that pile BA responsibilities on top of developer responsibilities might be intriguing if you have a coding background. They can be a good transition, but like a product manager, be prepared for the focus of your activities to be elsewhere. Gathering and writing requirements will not be your main goal. Writing code will be.

A final note on blends
With any blend you need to be proactive in obtaining the business analysis experiences that you want. We have a tendency toward the familiar. If you enter into a blend role with a strong background in the complementary skill set, you will have a strong tendency to leverage your prior experience instead of truly learn the business analysis ropes.

In many organizations today, roles and responsibilities are getting shifted between teams and positions. This is especially true in organizations employing agile processes. These ways of building software throw most of the traditional roles out the window, leaving room for individuals to craft new roles or customize roles to suit their strengths and career goals. Finding the right position and starting your business analysis career is more about what you are doing to gain experience than what your title is.

Putting it to Practice # 18

Start a BA position criteria-list
Given the types of positions, start a list of criteria for your potential position. Consider the following:

- Would you accept a contract position?
- Would you accept a temporary position?
- What proximity does the office need to be from your home?
- How often are you will to travel?
- What are your salary expectations (hourly and annually)?
- What are your expectations of benefits (healthcare, vacation time, personal time, etc)?
- What blends would you consider?

WHAT MAKES A JOB A BA JOB?

Not all BA jobs come right out and tell you that you are going to be a business analyst. There are many positions involving significant BA responsibilities with other titles and there are jobs with the "business analyst" title but very few BA responsibilities.

Here's a quick list of questions gauge if a job is really a BA job. Determining if a job really involves business analysis is not always straight-forward. You'll need to read through the lines and often ask lots of questions.

- Are you responsible for eliciting requirements?
- Are you working with multiple stakeholders?
- Does this position require analysis?

- Will you be responsible for creating documentation as deliverables? [18]
- Will representatives from business and IT review, approve, and consume the documentation?
- Will you communicate with representatives from the business and IT side?
- Will you be involved in selecting, reviewing, and scoping the solution?

In general, a business analyst is in end-to-end role that is truly the liaison between the business and the technology team.

BUSINESS OR IT?

Another variation on the business analysis role involves the balance of Business and IT. Although the business analyst typically reports up to a hiring manager either on the business team or on the IT team, the role conceptually sits between the two. On the "business side" are the efforts to elicit and gather requirements and on the "IT side" is working with the implementation team to define the solution, problem solve, and validate the requirements.

---

[18] Often developer-type jobs are responsible for gathering requirements but not for analyzing or documenting them.

It is doubtful that any position maintains an exact balance. If you have multiple stakeholders, especially more than 3 or 4, you will probably spend more time working through business problems and aligning stakeholders around the scope of the solution. If you have a smaller set of stakeholders (or someone else takes care of managing multiple inputs) you might spend more time working on the system side and "working" the requirements into those of an existing system. If the implementation team has a strong architect or application development lead, they might be content with a strong set of business requirements and be able to work through the functional

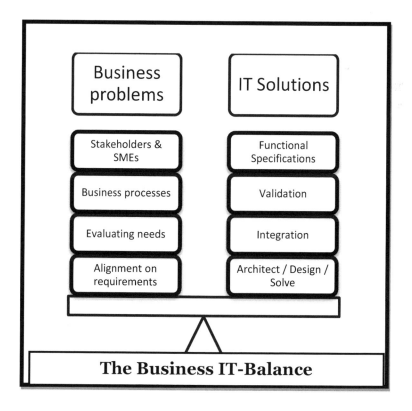

specifications with you serving as the stakeholder. [19]

But none of this represents any hard and fast rules...just be prepared for a wide variety and think about what you might enjoy most. Do you want to be more engaged with the business side, helping facilitate consensus and solve business problems? Do you want to work from a fairly defined set of business goals or objectives and facilitate the solution? No matter what the position, you should feel some pull from one side to the other as you help negotiate solutions to business problems.

Putting it to Practice # 19

Add some shape to your target position
Does anything in the above trigger new criteria your next position must fulfill? Add to your criteria list.

WHAT WILL YOUR NEXT POSITION BE?

No matter your situation, you have several options to consider.

Are you ready for a new BA position in a new organization?

When you go through the business analysis competencies in chapter 3 and the checklist above, do you feel well-qualified? Do you feel like you have been

---

[19] There is growing evidence that strong QA leads on an agile teams are taking on some of these responsibilities in working through the '"acceptance criteria" for product backlog items.

doing business analysis work all along and just calling it something else? Or, as you have been reading this book and doing your homework have you been able to take on so many business analysis responsibilities that you have essentially morphed it into a BA role? Both of these situations are entirely possible. The BA profession is still relatively new and there is a general lack of awareness about it. It's possible to be a BA without even knowing it.

If either the above scenarios is the case, you may indeed have the experience necessary to qualify yourself for a BA position, even a position outside your organization.

Can you find a BA position (or something close) within your current organization?

Barring the above situation, the easiest possible way to transition is to find a position within your current organization. Organizational knowledge is a key component of business analysis. At a new organization, you need to learn the basics of how things are organized, how information flows, and what tools are available. Taking on a new role is much easier when you are familiar with these underlying basics and, especially, if you will be working with many of the same people.

Does your current company have BAs? Are there open positions? If not, are there people who do BA work and would those positions be interesting to you?

If your organization does not have a formal BA role, would your organization benefit from implementing a BA practice? What would it look like to make a case for creating a new business analyst position? Is this something you can influence or pilot?

Can you leverage your industry experience?

After digging through your current company for opportunities and potential positions, the next place to look is for positions that leverage your industry experience or specific background. Do you have specific expertise that you can leverage to qualify yourself for a BA role?

Can you leverage related experience to take on a blended role?

Looking at the blends above do you have the requisite expertise to specifically seek out a blended role? Do you have the focus and persistence necessary to work outside your comfort zone and obtain the BA experiences necessary to qualify yourself for a full-fledged business analysis position?

Do you need to take an intermediate step?

If none of these opportunities present themselves to you, it might be that where you are now and where you want to go are so disparate that your best move in the short-term is to take an intermediate step toward a BA role. Look for jobs for which your previous experience qualifies you but that also have some key business analysis characteristics, giving you the transitional experience that you need to secure your dream job a year or two down the road.

Throughout my research for this book as well as Q&A in various online forums, I've discovered that there are a variety of career paths to business analysis. There is no one right or best intermediate role. The right role for you will depend highly on your prior experience and your specific career roles. That said, roles that offer opportunities to accumulate BA-type experiences and expose you to software development,

---

Transitional Roles

"When you are looking for a transitional role, you need to be prepared for possibly taking a cut in pay or even lower level position in the organizational hierarchy to gain exposure to software projects and the experience needed to make the change. It is also very important to educate your network. Let them know this is a career change and you know it, and let them know specifically the types of jobs you are seeking that will put you on the right track. Don't assume they will know what these jobs are!"

-Lori Lister, formerly: IT recruiter, currently: project coordinator, career goal: business analyst

while tending to require less experience, include the following:

- Software tester
- Project coordinator
- Assistant role to a CIO or other technology executive
- Technical writing
- Technical training
- Technical support[20]

Should you continue building BA experiences in your current situation?

It may be that the best possible way to become a business analyst is staying right where you are at and continuing to build BA experiences. If you have a good manager who is willing to give you flexible assignments and maybe even a little coaching, this could be the right choice.

Putting it to Practice # 20

Discover what you bring to the table

This is the time to do some hard thinking and figure out where your knowledge, experiences, and tolerance for risk put you in terms of the above options. What options are open to you as you are today? What

---

[20] For 10 stories from individuals about their career path, check out the discussion titled "What was your path to BA?"on the BA Forum on LinkedIn. You must join the group to view the discussion. This discussion thread was started in December of 2008, so you will need to search to find it.

options could you qualify yourself for in the next few months?

If you are unable to be brutally honest with yourself, seek the advice of someone who can be honest with you, such as a mentor or your manager.

Putting it to Practice # 21

Set a clear intention—Choose your target position
Unfortunately, there is not much in the way of general advice on this topic. The decisions you make here will be highly personal and extremely dependent on your current situation. My best advice is to pause, consider, reflect, talk to people, and consider your decisions some more.

Up to this point, the entire book and set of tasks has been about turning your mind toward your goal of being a business analyst and offering various frameworks for achieving this goal. Some have probably worked for you and others not.

Now is the time to set a path out for yourself. Take this "turning of the mind" a step farther and really envision what you want for yourself out of this new career. Define as clearly as you can what your target position will look like. You might choose to detail out multiple target positions, some you are qualified for now and some you know you want to pursue in the future. You may want to sift through the job descriptions you've been collecting as they can help you define potential responsibilities you'd like to incorporate into your next position.

Consider what it will look like, what it will feel like. Think about how you will run a meeting, prepare documentation, and even what you will wear to work. Focusing your mind on this intention opens up possibilities in the world around you.

Be aware of them.

Chapter 7

Finding a business analysis job

In this chapter we will cover the basics of job hunting for a business analyst or transitional role. To find your target position, you will need to be armed with an updated resume, some job search and evaluation techniques, and, of course, be expertly prepared for phone and in-person interviews.

This section is not intended to be a complete "finding a job" resource, but instead to augment those resources with tools, tips, and techniques specifically targeted to someone finding a job in the BA profession.

Good luck!

UPDATE YOUR RESUME

Focus on outcomes, not responsibilities

Most people produce resumes that focus on detailed job responsibilities over the history of their career. Typical resumes like this have many limitations, mostly in that they focus on roles and activities instead of outcomes. They limit your ability to sell yourself. If you were applying for a job you've done before, this kind of resume could get your foot in the door. But you are most likely going to be applying for a job you've never done before or that you've done in bits and pieces by taking on activities outside of your job description.

Instead of detailing your responsibilities consider an outcome- or achievement-based resume. This type of resume lists your achievements in each position and focuses on outcomes relevant to the job for which you are applying. Quite honestly, someone that is hiring you into a title that you've never done before does not care about all the other things you've done. They care most about what you've achieved and what you can do for them. Put yourself in your hiring manager's shoes. What would make them feel confident in spending some of their valuable time to bring you into an interview?

What kinds of outcomes should you list in a resume?

First, focus on any outcomes that had a material impact on your organization. Did you increase sales, increase operational efficiency, find new clients, reduce a specific kind of issue? The point here is to quantify what you did in terms of impact to the company. A good hiring manager will see this pattern of contribution and understand what it means you can do for their team and organization.

Second, focus on changes you made happen. Did you increase test coverage by X%? Did you release a new Intranet? Did you introduce a new tool or process?

If you are having trouble with this try to first brainstorm all the possible outcomes without any consideration for what will make it into your final resume. Another way to get to outcomes is to look at the tasks you did and ask "what did I accomplish by that?" or "what difference did I make?" or "why did I do it that way?"

When you have developed a list of outcomes, quantify them with numbers. How many people did you work with? How much money did you save? How many hours were saved? Be specific. Was the team of people local or remote?

Putting it to Practice # 22

Create a list of outcomes
In this exercise, you'll create the input you need for a stellar outcomes-based resume for your target position.

1. Pull out your list of BA experiences. All that journaling you have done to learn from your BA experiences now has added value—you have all kinds of input for your new resume!
2. For each experience, consider the outcome you helped your organization or team achieve. What difference did you make?
3. Pull out your old resume. Mine it for outcomes and achievements. If your old resume is activity-focused, use the activities to generate ideas for more outcomes and achievements.
4. Review your list of outcomes. Keep adding to your list until you've exhausted all your ideas.

Optimizing your resume

Trigger interview questions you want to answer
Another objective of a resume is to create good interview questions. The immediate purpose of your resume is to get you an interview but the underlying purpose is to get you a job. Many interviewers use

> *"I customized my resume to reflect qualifications for business analyst jobs that I had done in some fashion in my career."*
>
> *-Doug Hill, found his first BA job as a Senior Business Analyst (with 10 years of IT experience with some BA responsibilities and 2 degrees)*

your resume as a resource in the interview and pick out what they want to know more about. Give them some good questions to ask by highlighting experiences that you can speak to in detail. For every bullet in your resume be prepared with supporting details or a story about an experience that brings your professional personality to life.

Focus on BA-related achievements

By now, you are probably starting to see how some achievements can look a lot more like business analyst experiences than they already have. You'll want to work these experiences into prominent places within your resume as "accomplishments" for each position or in a general accomplishments section at the top of the resume.

An outcome-based resume also allows you to tweak things in your favor by using BA terms to describe outcomes you achieved. Did you help your company select a bug tracking tool? Did you list out the features you wanted? Did you interview others to determine what they wanted out of a tool? Sounds a lot like requirements elicitation and analysis to me. Review the job descriptions you've been saving and scan them for terms. You should talk about what you've actually done using the terms that employers are using to find candidates.

You might feel that this is being dishonest. Believe me, I am not encouraging you to be dishonest or even to stretch the truth. Everything in your resume should reflect what you have actually done. There is absolutely nothing wrong with rephrasing what you did as long as you are honest about what the outcome was and your role in it. Rephrasing responsibilities in the language used by the industry (as opposed to the language of the company you are/were in) is not a lie nor is it stretching the truth. It's talking the talk.

You might consider including other accomplishments as well, especially if they had a significant impact on your organization. Not everything has to be "BA" and you don't want to understate your abilities by excluding all irrelevant experience. But take care to keep the focus on accomplishments related to a your target position.

Putting it to Practice # 23

Prune your Outcomes List
Pull out the outcomes list you worked on earlier in this chapter. Now is the time to be more critical of what makes it into your resume vs. what does not.

1. First read through the list and see if you can think of anything else to *add*.
2. Go through the list and highlight any outcomes that related to a BA experience or your target intermediate experience.
3. For each outcome, see if you can incorporate some BA catch phrases to describe how you achieved the outcome. Did you elicit functional requirements? Create a gap analysis? Interview business stakeholders? Drive consensus? Run a meeting? You get the idea.
4. Go back through this refined list and highlight any that you feel like you could talk about in depth.

Handling the "roles and responsibilities"
What do I do with my roles and responsibilities? Some people choose to list accomplishments and responsibilities. If you had a leadership position or an ambiguous job title with a lot of responsibilities, this might be necessary. If at all possible, I recommend briefly summarizing the job position in a one or two line sentence underneath and using the bulk of resume space to highlight accomplishments related to your target position. No one cares that you got coffee for the executive, produced a monthly report, or managed the time sheet process. They care that you

know how to influence your superiors, can help align an executive team around a technology road map, and implemented a change to increase the accuracy of your project cost reporting (if, in fact, you did these things). If you did web development, database work, or any other technical task that is not part of the job description you are applying for, it might best to state these only briefly or leave them off completely.

A word (or two or three) on job titles
One of the biggest hurdles to creating an achievement-based resume can be that your titles and accomplishments just don't fit together all that well. When you go back through your outcomes, you might feel like these accomplishments seem circumspect given the title you had at the time. As I talked to people going through career transitions, I found that many people chose to make-up new titles that reflected the actual work they were doing or supplement their real title with a more descriptive one in parentheses.

Personally I've addressed this situation using the parentheses idea and by using a brief sentence or two to highlight my responsibilities in a way that makes sense of the title, description, and accomplishments. There are probably as many solutions to this problem as there are individuals out there applying for jobs. Just be aware that there is room to be flexible in your job titles.

If you are flexible with your job titles in your resume, be sure to inform your references. If a potential employer contacts someone, they are likely to reference the title on your resume. Be sure your reference understands how you are presenting that position and are comfortable supporting that characterization so they don't mistakenly botch a reference-check.

Putting it to Practice # 24

Update your Resume
Using your new list of outcomes, rework your resume into an outcome-based resume. Include the outcomes you starred in a prominent position to help ensure they are noticed and trigger the questions you want to answer.

Ask at least 2-3 people review it and provide feedback before sending it to a recruiter or hiring manager.

REFERENCES

Many employers will ask to check your references. These requests often come on short notice. As you start your job search, begin compiling your references list. Contact each potential reference personally to ask their permission to use them as a reference, confirm their contact information, and explain your target position.

Ideally you want to build a list of potential references that is longer than you need so you can select the 2 or 3 most appropriate references for a specific position.

Consider including the following types of people on your list:

- Current or former managers
- Anyone you worked with on the "business" side to elicit requirements
- Anyone you worked with on the "technical" side to implement requirements
- Business analysts with whom you've worked
- Trainers, mentors, or others who understand your potential capabilities as a business analyst.

Related to references, it is commonplace for job seekers to request recommendations on LinkedIn. Recommendations appear on your profile and often provide co-workers with opportunities to say how much they enjoyed working with you or express a unique perspective of your talents. Consider customizing your request for recommendations by explaining the types of positions you are looking for and asking people to highlight their experiences with you that would best apply to your target position. When seeking recommendations you can cast a broader net and include formal co-workers at all levels.

Putting it to Practice # 25

Develop a references list

Get a head start on your references list. Identify a target list of references and begin communicating with them about being a reference. This can also be a great opportunity to touch base about potential opportunities of which they might be aware or to seek advice on your career path. Keep your list ready at hand and nicely formatted. You'll never know when you need it.

WORK SAMPLES

On occasion a hiring manager will request work samples. What are hiring managers looking for when they ask for work samples? Managers are looking for proof that you can do what you say you can do. It's one thing to talk about a use case, it's another to show them a use case you created. If a specific methodology is critical to a position, they might ask for deliverables that fit within that methodology.   Otherwise the request might be more generic.

As a hiring manager, I've also had candidates bring

Career Management Tip

Don't be caught by surprise if you are escorted out the door during an unexpected layoff without any of your files. Save your work off into a personal storage device at least once every six months. In addition to providing work samples, your files can help you trigger accomplishments for your resume.

work samples with them to an interview and get them out when I asked a question about a specific deliverable. This often created a favorable impression of the candidate, especially if the example was relevant and they could speak in detail to how they created it.

If you were able to take on any BA type tasks, the deliverables you created as part of these tasks are obviously the best candidates for work samples. Go through them and clean them up so that none of the information exposes anything about the company that would be inappropriate or violate a non-disclosure agreement.

See if you can't create 3-4 samples to meet different situations. Examples include:

- Requirements document / features list
- Use Case
- Diagram
- User story or acceptance test
- UI mock-up or wireframe

A note on samples: Do not try to cheat or copy something off the Internet. A good interviewer will ask you to talk in detail about the sample and ask you questions about how you created the sample. Be prepared to talk through how you took "nothing" and created "something" from the initial assignment through to the delivered end product. Good managers know that a deliverable itself is not nearly as important as the process you went through to create it and the sum value it provided to your organization.

If you are at a loss for samples, go back to the fun tips for integrating business analysis into your personal life and create one. An honest sample showing personal initiative to learn the ropes is better than none at all or one hacked from the internet.

Another idea is to create a sample for a specific job. If their product is available on the web or for a free download, go through and document a use case or diagram for a feature as you were able to experience it via their product. For an added kick, interview someone you know who uses the product or a competitive product and elicit their "wish list" of features.

Putting it to Practice # 26

Prepare a set of work samples
Use the guidelines above or your personal experiences to prepare a few work samples illustrating the business analysis experiences you have accumulated so far. Remove any information that might be considered confidential or proprietary. Practice speaking to how and why you created these deliverables.

THE JOB SEARCH

Using job boards

Now that you've got a resume highlighting your professional achievements, it's time to get it out in front of the people who are in a position to hire you. There tens of thousands of job boards and applying for jobs you find online could be a full-time job. You will need to take some time on a day you are feeling very patient and set-up profiles on several job boards. Consider the following job boards that more targeted toward the BA profession:

- Dice (http://www.dice.com): a job board that specializes in technology jobs.
- IIBA Career Center (http://www.theiiba.org/careers): an international job board site focusing specifically on jobs for business analyst.
- http://www.bajob.ca/ -- specific to business analyst jobs in Canada.

To find the latest on niche job boards in the software space, check out the following resource: http://www.quintcareers.com/computer_jobs.html

It is also a good idea to post your resume and search for jobs on a few "general" job boards. Finding relevant jobs on these sites will be more difficult because of the breadth of job postings, but you will likely find jobs not posted other places.

- http://www.monster.com
- http://www.careerbuilder.com

If Craigslist (http://www.craigslist.com) supports your location it can be a great way to find jobs at smaller companies that might not post on the big job boards.

Most locations also have job boards specific to user groups or other local groups. You'll find these resources by asking the people you meet networking.

Finally, consider including job board aggregators in your search. These sites aggregate jobs from multiple job boards and can provide a more efficient way to search (you'll likely have to set-up a resume/profile to apply to jobs on individual sites).

> Business Analysis job descriptions keywords:
>
> - Liaison
> - Translate
> - Deliverables
> - Communicate
> - Artifacts
> - Collaborate
> - Requirements
> - Specifications
> - Design
> - Facilitate
> - Elicit
> - Organized
> - Analytical
> - Systems-focused

- http://www.simplyhired.com
- http://www.indeed.com

Position Titles

Not all jobs with "business analyst" in the title are really BA jobs. And, likewise, not all BA roles have a title of "business analyst". Our profession is still relatively ill-defined and misunderstood. There are also business analyst jobs in the financial industry that focus on financial analysis. This alternative use of the title adds to the confusion.

Given this reality, it's worthwhile to extend your search beyond jobs titled "business analyst". Concern yourself more with the details of the job description than the title. But when searching job boards, titles are important, so here's a set to consider:

- Business systems analyst
- Computer analyst
- IT business analyst
- Business process engineer
- Product manager
- Product owner
- Requirements manager or engineer
- Requirements analyst
- Systems analyst
- Information architect
- Development manager or lead
- Data analyst or architect
- Project manager (many PM jobs have significant BA responsibilities)
- Technical project manager
- Technical product manager

- Implementation manager, specialist, or engineer
- Project coordinator
- SCRUM master
- Product coordinator (these are often assistants to the product manager and occasionally involve dealing with the product development details or liaising with the IT team)

Most positions with these titles will probably not be BA positions. But they could be or they could be blended positions. Expanding your titles could help you find positions that others are missing.

But how am I really going to find a position?
Career experts tell us that most positions are never officially posted and that many positions are filled by leveraging personal and professional relationships, not online postings and applications. This is why it is so important to forge relationships with other business analysts and industry professionals. Not to say you should not work the online job market, but if you are in a position currently, it might be a better use of your time to post your resume on a few targeted boards, sign-up for weekly email alerts to stay informed about what is available, apply to jobs that capture your intense interest, but spend the bulk of your time networking. If you are unemployed, you likely have the time to be comprehensive with the online and offline aspects of your search. Just remember the odds are that your relationship-building activities will be more productive over time

> *"You can't depend on your network to get you a job. You need to find the jobs your network can help you get."*
>
> **-Lori Lister, Current Project Coordinator / Future Business Analyst**

than applying for jobs posted by people that you do not know.

Your professional networking might also help you get an "in" to a job you find posted online. When applying to jobs online, don't hesitate to also follow-up with any contacts you have that might be able to give you an insight into the job requirements and be in a position to formally recommend you. Regardless of how much you stay in front of people, you will likely uncover opportunities they knew about but just never thought to bring to your attention. It's important not to assume that they know you would be a fit for the position or even interested. In fact, they may not even know about the opening.

When networking for a position balance subtlety with persistence. It is common that people will forget about you and your search so you want to stay top of mind. Reconnect at meetings and with the occasional email.

Working with Recruiters
Recruiters present an interesting option for a new business analyst. A recruiter's goal is to present well-

qualified candidates to potential employers. Employers use recruiters either because they do not have the time to sift through job applications for qualified candidates or because they are searching for a unique skill set and need help marketing their open position. A recruiter gets paid for placing a candidate in a position so they only get a commission if you are hired as a full-time employee or by shaving a margin off an hourly rate if you are a contractor. In a contract-to-hire situation, a recruiter might get paid both an hourly margin and a conversion fee when you are hired.

Most often recruiters work with employers to understand their job openings and the details of the position. Some recruiters also try to understand the company and team culture and develop a deeper understanding of what the employer really needs in an employee. Recruiters then actively recruit for candidates to present for the position. Sometimes recruiters work from their own candidate pools that they develop through networking and resume submissions. Oftentimes recruiters will also post positions to job boards to seek additional applicants. It's very possible to have multiple recruiters working the same employer and the same position.

When the recruiter is satisfied that a candidate is qualified for a position, they will present that candidate to their contact at the employer. When submitting your resume to a recruiter, you want to make sure that they will contact you for your permission before submitting your resume. If you are working with multiple recruiters you want to avoid having your resume submitted to the same employer multiple times. Recruiters often present a customized version of your skill summary, possibly by editing your resume to highlight key experiences or with a detailed "cover letter". You may experience a recruiter who goes beyond highlighting and tries to doctor your resume. Never support a recruiter presenting you as something you are not and run away from any recruiter who does.

As you are starting your job search, consider speaking with a few local recruiters. To find the most reputable recruiters in your industry and local area, ask your contacts and informational interviewees for recommendations. If nothing else, speaking with recruiters will help you get a feel for how your skill set stacks up against the candidate competition. But do know that recruiters are less likely to take a chance on presenting you unless you have a specific expertise that uniquely qualifies you for a position (industry, tool, process, etc.), especially in a tight economy with a saturated candidate pool. In positive economies where the available jobs outnumber the candidates, recruiters might be willing to present you and help you sell your previous experience, but oftentimes at a lower hourly rate. In general, recruiters are judged by the quality of the candidates they present and need a reason to take a risk on a new BA.

Putting it to Practice # 27

Get searching and applying!
Explore the resources above to initiate your search. As you find positions you are qualified for (or are on the brink of qualifying for) apply! Write a custom cover letter for each position, highlighting the experiences you have that directly correlate to the position description. It might not hurt to include a note about why you want to be a business analyst and summarize the work you have done to qualify yourself for the role.

Applying to jobs requires a balance between quantity and quality. When in doubt, focus on quality applications: jobs you are qualified for, interested in, and apply for with high-touch, customized cover letters. For an even higher-quality application, create a customized version of your resume to highlight experiences relevant to the specific position.

PREPARING FOR THE INTERVIEW

Outside a good resume, preparing for an interview is one of the most impactful activities you can do to land a promising position. It is important to be confident and calm. Interviews are a way to find out more about the potential opportunity as well as share why you believe yourself to be an ideal candidate.

A business analyst is such a core role on a project or within an organization, you will often interview with multiple individuals, likely including people within the IT group and within the business group. Be prepared by anticipating the perspective of the hiring manager and other interviewers, bringing questions to ask, and practicing talking about your BA experiences.

Perspective of the hiring manager

Consider carefully the perspective of the hiring manager. Find out what you can about their background and the breadth of their responsibilities. Attempt to ascertain their pain points, whether through "reading between the lines" of the job description, asking people you know at the company, or asking questions through the interview process. There is no one-size-fits-all view of a hiring manager, but there are some general guidelines that might help you hypothesize their perspective.

If the hiring manager is in the IT group, you will be their primary contact with the customer, alongside some people in other key roles such as project manager. Business analysts often work fairly independently, so the manager needs to trust that you will be a good communicator, will be proactive, will learn quickly, and come to them with any issues. Most importantly, they want to know you will communicate, communicate, communicate and then, communicate some more. And that this communication will not be the bowl people over type of communication but the open, honest, and collaborative style that will help all people on the team shine. You will have a critical role in shaping the business's perception of IT by setting realistic expectations, asking questions and doing the analysis that ensures IT can deliver on its promises.

If the hiring manager is within a business group, they are probably bringing you in to help keep their communication with IT organized. You might be helping facilitate alignment across a variety of business stakeholders or working with the main stakeholder (likely the hiring manager) to see his or her vision through to implementation. They are likely looking to find someone who can help IT accomplish the objectives of their specific business unit or project team. You need to prove to them that you will be able to understand their goals and objectives but also that you can serve up these objectives in ways that the development team can understand and, most importantly, act on. People on the business side are often tired of hearing "it's a requirement issue" or "I didn't know what to do". Especially if this is a new position, they want to know that you'll handle the IT communication on their behalf.

Some other aspects of the hiring manager's perspective could include:

- Is this a new position? Is there a BA team in place? If so, they will want to know how your skills will save them time in whatever communication issues they are currently dealing with and also that you can bring experience from different kinds of projects to build a process that will work best within their organizational dynamic.

- Will you be part of an established team with a formal process? If so, they will be looking for you to be knowledgeable in the basics of their methodology (to the extent it's publicly available) and possibly the tools they use. They may want to be sure you are willing to work within their process.

What questions will they ask? Most BA interviews I've participated in as a manager or candidate and spoken with others about involve more situational-based questions than technical ones. This is not to say that your technical skills are not important, they are just not as important as your ability to communicate, facilitate, and help people solve problems.

Hiring managers want to understand how you will approach different situations that you will face in their

---

"Make a connection with your hiring manager. People want to work with competent, skilled people...but equally they want to work with people that they like and want to work with.

A hiring manager should walk away saying 'I can't wait to talk to that person again!'"

-Doug Hill, Senior Business Analyst.

organization. How do you help people prioritize? How do you handle people who go off-topic in meetings? How do you approach change?

Often a hiring manager will often want you to talk through one or two projects you've worked on, especially those that involved the relevant responsibilities you list on your resume. Be prepared to speak specifically to what you did and how you achieved specific objectives. List the deliverables you created, the meetings you organized, and the people you interviewed. Talk about how you managed the discussions and be specific with examples whenever you can. Because the BA role is facilitative by nature, many interviewees tend to talk about what "we" did. While it is great to be a team player and you want that attitude to shine through, in an interview situation be very clear about what *you* contributed.

Perspectives of other interviewers
Very often you will not only interview with your hiring manager, but also with individuals across the project team.

Other business analysts
Most hiring managers with an existing BA team will bring in one or more business analysts into the interview process. Other business analysts will want to gauge how you'll fit in with the team and organizational culture. One or more of them may be a senior BA who could potentially be overseeing your day-to-day work and mentoring you in the role. Within any team, there will be various perspectives.

Common perspectives include:

- **Process orientation**. Do you know what you say you do about a specific deliverables or methodology?
- **Tool orientation.** Do you know what you say you do about a specific system, industry, or requirements tool?
- **Inter-personal orientation.** Do you have the skills necessary to deal with the more challenging personalities they work with on either the business or implementation team? Questions like "How do you handle someone who goes off topic in a meeting" or "Tell me about a time when you negotiated a solution with a developer" might be looking for specific inter-personal experiences.
- **Team orientation.** Are you flexible? Are you going to learn their existing process before suggesting radical changes? Do you bring a new perspective that adds value? Will you be cooperative?

Developers and Development Managers
Most developers who have been in their profession for more than a few years have been burned at least once by bad requirements or the complete lack of a business analyst. They will want to make sure they do not get burned by you. But developers also want to be involved in the process, so look for questions that are gauging if you are going to cut them out of the loop and micro-manage them through your requirements.

Developers want to participate in the requirements process, but most prefer not to own it.

Quality Assurance Engineers and QA Managers
Like developers, QA engineers want to make sure they do not get burned by bad requirements. QA people will probably be looking for more detail and precision. They want your requirements to be testable and give them a clear indication by which they can evaluate whether or not everything is working as expected. QA professionals often want to be involved in the requirements process and have the opportunity to provide feedback.

Business SMEs
Business subject matter experts might be product managers, marketing managers, or internal process owners from any function within the company. Some business SMEs have been doing the BA job (if this is a new role) or have been suffering from a lack of support (if you are replacing someone who left). They want to understand how you are going to obtain their perspective and how involved they will be. Business SMEs can run the gamut from people who want very little direct involvement and will just be glad to have someone to talk to the techies for them to those who want complete control and see your role as cutting them off from direct contact with the implementation team.

Project Managers
There can be a lot of varying perspectives from project managers. Schedule-driven PMs will ask about your

planning skills and how quickly you can get things done. They are often on a deadline before you are even hired, so efficiency is a key value to them. They will want to know how you help the business prioritize new requests as well as manage scope. The business analyst often has a lot of indirect influence over the scope of a project. They also help minimize risk through their proactive analysis. A good BA is a project manager's best friend. An inadequate BA throws the brunt of their inadequacy on the project manager who often is forced to step in to fill the gap.

Human Resources

At a larger company, every candidate is interviewed by a representative from human resources. Sometimes a human resources professional performs the initial interview for screening purposes. This can be a challenge for a new business analyst, because like recruiters, HR professionals like to pass on qualified candidates. But unlike IT-focused recruiters, HR professionals may have a limited perspective of the business analyst role. These interviews tend to focus on the specific job position qualifications or on personality and organizational fit.

Questions to ask

An interview should not be a one way street. You should be given ample opportunity to ask questions and some interviewers will judge you more by your questions than your answers. Your questions could be perceived as evidence of your interviewing and listening skills and your analytical abilities.

Be prepared with the following types of questions:

- **Business model**. Ask detailed questions that show you understand the business and have thought about it. Do a little analysis...how does the company generate revenue? What are its highest value services? How does technology support or constrain those efforts?
- **Projects**. What kind of projects will you be working on? What is the strategic impact of those projects? How does the project fit into the larger objectives of the organization? What do they hope to achieve?
- **Expectations**? What will an ideal candidate look like? What are the expectations of someone in this role? What kind of support will I have? Product knowledge is important, how will I be able to learn about the product?
- **Culture**. What is the team like? How do people work together? What do you like about working here? What's your least favorite thing about working here?
- **Process**. Find out what is in place in terms of a software development process and what your role will be within it.
- **Systems**. Ask questions about the tools and technologies the organization uses to support the process and the product.

Preparation: General

At this point you have already updated your resume and hopefully included trigger points for conversations about your past experience. The most important thing you can do to prepare for an interview is think through (and talk through) several experiences you have accumulated that represent your talents and skills. Remember most of the questions you get are meant to gauge your inter-personal and situational talents above your technical skills.

Consider all the outcome-based experiences you put on your resume. Write in detail what you specifically did to achieve those outcomes. Who did you talk to? What strengths did you bring? What deliverables did you create? What could you have done better? You can never expect yourself to be specifically prepared for each and every interview question, but if you have thought through some key experiences most often one or more of them will apply to the question you are asked.

If you want to prepare for specific questions and also learn to "talk the talk" the Modern Analyst site also has a comprehensive list of potential interview questions that have been built by the BA community:

http://modernanalyst.com/Careers/InterviewQuestions/tabid/128/Default.aspx

Preparation: Specific Position

Once you have an interview scheduled for a specific position, it is a good idea to prepare specifically for that interview. If the job description listed specific technical skills, you should be prepared to answer questions about these skills and provide examples of your experiences. For example, if the job description indicates that the business analysts document requirements in use cases, be prepared with what a definition of a use case is. You can research this on the web or read a book. You might even want to create a sample (in your work if possible, otherwise in your personal life) to show some initiative in learning the technical skills you'll need for the job. Some managers might ask you to define it but others will go a step beyond. I used to ask candidates what they saw as the limitations of a use case, thereby assessing their understanding of the technique and their ability to use it in context.

If you really do not have experience with a technical skill that is required (or asked of you), the very best thing you can do when asked these types of questions is be humble about what you know, how you researched your topic, and then shift the conversation..."I'm a quick learner and I found that XYZ book was recommended. If I get this position, I'd plan to purchase that book and study it along with hopefully some mentoring from the more senior people on the team."

The Simulation

It is possible that a potential employer will ask you to simulate being a business analyst in an interview. These interview techniques are designed to test your aptitude to really do the job and not just talk about doing the job. They also provide a hiring manager with a sense of your personal poise as well as how you deal with pressure situations.

For example, the interviewer might ask you to elicit requirements about a feature and then document them. Or, they might have you lead them through a problem-solving session or elicitation session. For example, in a recent interview scenario, a hiring manager asked me to elicit requirements from someone playing the role of Bill Gates about a bathroom redesign. There is not much you can do to prepare. If you've accumulated legitimate BA experiences, are a fit for this role, and maintain your composure, you should do fine. The most important thing is to remain relaxed and confident.

Bad interviewers

One important thing that many candidates do not realize is that not all interviewers are good at interviewing. Just like there are bad candidates there are also bad interviewers. This may be due to inexperience, lack of preparation, or just someone who is poor at their job. You might have an interview where they never ask you a question, spend the entire time talking about how horrible the position is, or ask you irrelevant questions. In the face of these situations, stay as positive as possible. Look for ways to redirect your answers or general conversation to incorporate your experience stories. Make the best of it and hope this person does not have a lot of influence over the hiring decision or that you manage to impress them regardless of your perspective of the experience.

Some final tips

Never, ever say anything negative about your previous employer or job situation. An insightful hiring manager will infer the truth and respect your discretion. Many managers prompt for negative experiences because they want to avoid hiring negative people.

Be prepared to think big picture. Hiring managers are looking for BAs who will think outside the box. Even though you might be gathering requirements for a specific project, understanding the implications of what you learned on future projects can provide a lot of value. I used to ask "What are some of the things you feel the company could have done better?" I was looking for people with a positive attitude toward change and a broad perspective.

As a new business analyst, it's important to prepare diligently for interviews. You want to prepare and practice until you feel you can speak naturally about your qualifications. There is, of course, a danger of over-preparing, in that your answers might sound memorized or manufactured. The line is gray. It's best not to wing it, but also not to manufacture it.

Putting it to Practice # 28

Prepare for the interview: get your stories straight
This task is designed specifically to help you develop some natural conversations for your interviews. To do

this, you'll want to practice telling stories about your business analysis experiences. It might be helpful for you to first write out these stories in your own language. Then review these stories and compare them with keywords from the job descriptions you have collected. See if you can incorporate those words into your stories in a natural way. (If it feels awkward, you will be better off to keep with your own language.)

Once you land an interview for a specific position, consider going through this same activity, mining keywords from the position description.

EVALUATING AN OFFER

If you are persistent with the above, consistently explore your options and prepare, prepare, prepare, eventually a business analysis or transition-to-BA opportunity will become yours for the taking. But before taking the plunge on this new role, consider whether or not it is truly the right position for you.

Assess the cultural fit

You want to work a place that is a fit for you personally as well as professionally. Did you have the opportunity to meet with people you will be working with? Setting aside the natural discomfort of interviewing (for you and them), did you feel comfortable with them? Do these people seem to enjoy their jobs and passionate about what they are doing or are they bored, frustrated, and ready to quit.

Here are some questions to ask to get a feel for the culture.

- Why is this role open?
- What are your expectations of someone in this role?
- How do people work together here?
- What kind of processes do you have in place?

In addition to the people you'll be working with, you'll want to consider the cultural fit of the workplace as a whole.

- Is it formal or informal?
- What kind of attire is considered appropriate?
- Is it an open environment or one where people are closed?
- Is the organization charitable? Does it promote volunteer work?
- Will the company culture support your personal goals for work-life balance (i.e., flex-time, work-from-home, vacation time, etc.)?
- Are there other aspects of the culture that are important for you?

Assess personality fit with your manager

In most organizations, your relationship with your manager is one of the most fundamental to your overall satisfaction in the position. While you do not want to put the cart ahead of the horse in the interview, there are parts of the interview that begin to frame that relationship.

It is worthwhile to consider some of the "best" and "worst" bosses you have had in the past. Reflect on what made them the best and the worst from your perspective. During most interviewing processes, you will meet with the manager more than once. Use subsequent opportunities to ask deeper questions and get to know your potential manager better.

Some questions to consider:

- What are your expectations of a business analyst?
- How would you oversee my work?
- How do you provide feedback to your employees?
- What kind of support will I have?
- What's your management style?

There are not necessarily right and wrong answers to these questions. You need to be aware of your expectations of a manager and do your best to determine whether or not this new manager will be a good fit for you.

Frame this as a career opportunity

Every job change, whether within the same company or within a new one is an opportunity for you on many professional levels. You may have the opportunity to learn a new tool, gain experience in a marketable skill, or just plain get some experience.

Look back at all that you've done so far and figured out about where you want to be. How will this job help you get there? What gaps will it leave unfilled for you?

Some questions to consider:

- What will you learn?
- What marketable experience will you gain?
- Will you have access to any training?
- Will you have the support of a mentor or colleague to help you learn about business analysis?

Consider salary and benefits

Finally, consider the salary and benefits offered by the position. If you do not bring a lot of business analysis experience to the table, a salary cut may be necessary to find an entry-level business analysis position. In this case, you'll want to focus on how this position is a career opportunity for you. If you bring a lot of experience, especially in BA-type activities, to the table, you may be able to transition at a similar, or even higher, salary.

Regardless, be aware of what the fair market rate is for business analysts in your area. The IIBA recently published a salary survey in 2007 posted the results for their members [21] . Salary.com (http://www.salary.com) and The Glass Door

---

[21]

http://www.theiiba.org/AM/Template.cfm?Section=Roles&Template=/CM/HTMLDisplay.cfm&ContentID=4204

(http://www.theglassdoor.com)   are   also   good
resources for salary information.

What do you decide?

In the end, no one can make this decision for you.
Only you know your priorities and expectations. Make
a pros and cons list. Discuss the opportunity with a
close friend. Evaluate the upside and the downside.
Then listen to your gut.

CONCLUSION

I hope this book has helped you find your first business analyst position or started down the right path. If you are an over-achiever, you might knock out most of these activities in a few months. For others, you might spend a few years learning, growing, and gathering valuable experiences. There is no single path. You are not solving a puzzle. You are creating a new future career for yourself.

With each assignment you complete, you will learn something new. This changes you and sets you moving in a new direction. Whether or not you land the perfect business analysis job right away, trust that you are moving closer with each intentional step. No one can take these steps for you, but many are here to help you along your way.

ADDITIONAL RESOURCES

Free Email Newsletter from *Bridging the Gap*

Receive an email each Monday morning with a small action step for advancing your business analysis career.

http://www.bridging-the-gap.com/free-resources

Free Email Course on Becoming a BA

Stay motivated along your path with 8 emails over 4 weeks laying out the key steps to becoming a BA.

http://www.bridging-the-gap.com/enewsletter-sign-up/become-a-business-analyst-free-course/

Launching Your Business Analysis Career

A full-fledged virtual course with online instructor support to step you through each phase of becoming a business analyst, and help you break down whatever barriers are holding you back.

http://www.mybusinessanalysiscareer.com

LinkedIn Group: Starting a Business Analyst Career

Share your experiences, ask questions, and begin networking with other professionals facing similar career challenges.

http://www.linkedin.com/groups?gid=2012413

Author Online

For more resources about starting and advancing your business analyst career, visit the author at

www.bridging-the-gap.com

For Further Help

Laura Brandenburg provides BA training, consulting, and mentoring services and works with a network of coaches, trainers, and mentors to help BAs build fulfilling careers in business analysis.

Laura offers an online course, Launching Your Business Analysis Career that takes students step-by-step through the process laid out in this book with online instructor support.

Check out *Bridging the Gap* for information about current offerings or contact Laura at info@bridging-the-gap.com for more details.

6130694R00112

Made in the USA
San Bernardino, CA
02 December 2013